Landscapes of Britain

Landscapes of Britain

ROY MILLWARD and
ADRIAN ROBINSON

David & Charles Newton Abbot London North Pomfret (VT) Vancouver

ISBN 0 7153 7181 9

Library of Congress Catalog Card Number 76-55884

© Roy Millward and Adrian Robinson 1977

Printed in Great Britain
by Biddles of Guildford
for David & Charles (Publishers) Limited
Brunel House Newton Abbot Devon

Published in the United States of America
by David & Charles Inc
North Pomfret Vermont 05053 USA

Published in Canada
by Douglas David & Charles Limited
1875 Welch Street North Vancouver BC

Contents

Introduction

The variety of Britain's landscapes has long been proverbial among travellers in these islands. Three hours or less of motoring along the new trunk roads, M1 or M6, that lead northwards from the metropolis bring the traveller within sight of the hills of highland Britain. The Pennine wall rising westward of the motorway that cuts through the industrial squalor of the Derbyshire coalfield can look just as enticing as the first glimpse of the high Canadian Rockies seen from the monotonous prairie. The difference is one of scale. A thousand miles of prairie lead up to the Rockies; the regional differences of the British Isles are reckoned on a miniature scale in which a score of miles may encompass an immense variety of landscape features.

This wealth of interest contained in the scenery of the British Isles is to be measured not only in the range of scenic elements contained in the 900 miles (1,440km) that separate Lands End from John o'Groats; there is also the important element of time, and two time scales of very different dimensions are at once evident. Firstly, the composition and physical forms of the landscape, what some would call 'the natural landscape', have developed over a time scale that lies beyond the comprehension of mankind. It is possible to speculate about the immense span of the great geological epochs in which the rocks and structures of Earth were made and shaped, and nowadays refined techniques of analysis are leading towards a more exact computation of the great divisions of geological time, but the imagination cannot stretch to the comprehension of time units that contain hundreds of millions of years within which continents drifted across the face of Earth, mountain ranges were built and species of plants and animals evolved and became extinct. The shaping of the external lineaments of the landscape are part of a cosmic process, a process whose scale is so great that we in our short lives remain all but unaware of its working within contemporary time. Only an Andean earthquake or some new volcanic island, new-born from the depths of the Atlantic off Iceland, reveal the awesome mechanism beside which we live unknowing.

The history of man on Earth has given a second time scale to the shaping of the landscape. With a technology designed to provide shelter and extract the riches of the Earth, men have left their impression upon the face of the landscape ever since the first prehistoric farmers began the clearance of forests. The man-made landscape, one might almost say the hand-made landscape, owes its beginning to widely separated periods of time in different parts of the world. The ancient landscapes of the Middle East have borne the impression of human occupation for more than 10,000 years, but over a large part of America's Pacific North West man's effective subjugation of the wilderness did not begin until the twentieth century. In the British Isles the making of the landscape reaches through 5,000 years to the settlement of the first farmers — Neolithic colonists who brought from Europe the arts of agriculture and who made the earliest inroads into the woodlands of oak, elm, ash and hazel that covered the greater part of Britain. Before the Neolithic period — the thousand-year phase of British prehistory that is characterised by settled groups engaged in raising crops and livestock, building crude huts and making pottery — these islands were given over to a sparse population of hunters and fishermen, the men of the Mesolithic and Palaeolithic times whose economy made scarcely any impact on the natural landscape. Thus, from earlier than 3000BC man has engaged in the long and still unfinished process of shaping the British landscape, and today our scenery contains elements surviving from the many different culture phases of our island's history between the centuries of the Neolithic peasants and the motorway and television age in which we live.

The landscape is even suggestive of a continuity of use stretching far back into prehistory from our own times. The Icknield Way that follows the line of the chalk hills from Salisbury Plain to the salt-marsh-rimmed coastline of north Norfolk was certainly in existence at the time of the raising of Stonehenge in the twilight centuries of the late Neolithic. Likewise some of the mountain trails of highland Britain might well date back to prehistoric times. The lonely track that climbs across the long high ridge of High Street in the eastern Lake District may well originate in the same period of prehistory; later the Romans were to incorporate it in their own system of roads. And evidence is now forthcoming from intensive research by aerial photography over the river valleys of the Midlands — the Nene, Avon and Trent — of a long unsuspected ground-plan of prehistoric settlement beneath the present pattern of villages, lanes and hamlets. More than twenty years ago when Professor W. G. Hoskins showed in his book *The Making of the English Landscape* that the scenery of England has a long history as a result of man and his works, it seemed that the beginnings of that history lay with the Anglo-Saxons who made a vast and effective incursion into the natural forest cover of the lowlands and who were the founders of hundreds of villages and hamlets. As well as providing the elements of an English culture through their language and the foundations of a rural civilisation in lowland Britain, they established also the main features of England's landscapes. Two decades of research have now shown that the Anglo-Saxons entered a country in the fifth century where many landscape features had already been sketched out to serve men's purposes centuries earlier. The rampart-ringed enclosures of the Iron Age — the Iron-Age camps of our topographical maps, of which there are almost 3,000 still surviving in the British Isles — suggest a political and social order of the Celtic world that was

to be overwhelmed and transformed in the Saxon centuries. But the relics of this prehistoric Celtic Britain are still evident in the landscape: in the names of so many of our English rivers — Avon, Derwent, Severn, Thames to mention only a few; in the not so rare circular churchyards that suggest the adoption of a prehistoric pagan site for Christian worship; and in the emerging evidence, particularly in Dorset, Devon and East Anglia, that some field patterns and the shapes and boundaries of estates may be derived from the social and economic order of pre-Saxon times. As we look at the landscapes of Britain we begin to realise that a continuing evolution of scenery, in both a geological and a historical sense on vastly different scales of time, has produced the regional traits of our countryside that we know today.

This book represents an anthology of British landscape features. They have been chosen to illustrate some of the vital themes of the physical and social history of these islands. The opening pages, a geological posy rather than the replete and ordered surveys of the standard textbooks of British geology, exhibit specimens of the physical landscape selected from the long epochs through which our islands have been shaped. From the remote highlands of north-west Scotland the mountains of Suilven and Stac Polly, lonely natural fortresses of Torridonian Sandstone rising sheer from an ice-gnawed platform of Europe's oldest rocks, represent the first chapter of the physical development of Britain. Over the 2,000 million years that have elapsed since the making and shaping of Britain's oldest rocks in the Outer Hebrides many different geological materials have been added to the fabric of these islands. In that same long span of time climate has ranged from polar to tropical, continents have drifted, seas have flooded over and retreated, and volcanoes and mountains have erupted and uplifted only to be exposed to their very roots in subsequent long periods of erosion.

The different materials that compose

8

the varied fabric of Britain's landscape are discussed with illustrations from the cold gaunt Carboniferous Limestone plateau of the northern Pennines, the chalk hills of the South Downs with the dramatic line of vertical cliffs in the Seven Sisters, as well as the granite and gabbro roots of the Cuillin Hills — one of the chain of geologically recent volcanoes that form an intriguing rim to our western seaboard from Northern Ireland to the Hebrides. But the enjoyment of landscape is much more than an appreciation of colour and texture in different rocks. As our landscape poets and painters have always recognised, it is a composition of forms, architecture and sculpture on a grand scale wrought with nature's tools. Mountains above all are the great set pieces of this natural architecture. Ruskin was quick to compare the mountains of the Lake District to our great cathedrals; Scafell Pike with its vast cap of bare boulders above the eerie chasm of Mickledore may be classed as an example of Nature's 'gothic'.

The workings of wind, rain, rivers, waves and ice have resulted in the shaping of the present landscape. The marks of the Ice Age are the dominant imprint on the scenery of highland Britain in the knife-edged ridges that climb to the summit of Snowdon or in the long trench that cuts through the Cairngorm plateau. But the lowlands too owe many details of the physical scene to the events of the Quaternary Ice Age in the past 1¾ million years. Flat-floored valleys that cut through the low chalk hills of the Lincolnshire wolds were shaped by vanished Ice-Age rivers at a time when the landscape must have resembled the present-day braided, debris-filled valleys below the glacier plateaux of Iceland. Again, the vast accumulations of shingle at Hallsands in Devon, exploitation of which led to the destruction of a fishing village, were the legacy of the glacial period.

The shaping of the physical landscape is still taking place and some of the topics in the pages that follow refer to the great morphological processes that are still active and that can be measured through their effect upon our present environment. Holderness in Yorkshire, a coastline of low clay cliffs is, it has been claimed, the fastest eroding coast in the world. The lost medieval borough of Dunwich on the Suffolk coast vividly illustrates the effect of continuous erosion in historic times. Conversely, the silting and reclamation of the Wantsum Channel that centuries ago isolated the island of Thanet from mainland Kent erased what in Roman times had been an important line of sea communication between the Thames and the English Channel.

As already mentioned, the earliest recognisable phase of Man's interference with the natural processes of landscape evolution in the British Isles is marked by the Neolithic period, beginning in the fourth millenium BC when the first communities of farmers and stock rearers reached these shores. Man and his grazing animals were to achieve extensive clearances over the centuries of prehistory, clearances that are imprinted on so many tracts of Britain from the bare fells of Cumbria to the chalk downs that enclose the Weald. The fragments of heath that survive in the countryside of Greater London, and many more that are now remembered only in a placename, probably came into existence in the Bronze Age.

People possessed of only a simple technology have been able to change the face of the landscape largely through the clearing of woodland, but the economic demands of larger and more advanced communities in historic time have exercised a deeper and more destructive influence. For instance, the history of the Norfolk Broads, unravelled in the 1950s by the combined work of a geomorphologist, an historical geographer and a botanist, illustrates the power of a medieval community in the shaping of its natural surroundings. The Broads, once believed to be of physical origin, have been shown to have developed as a result of the flooding of medieval peat-diggings. Again, the eighteenth century marked the beginning of 200 years of steeply rising population in the British Isles and the introduction of a continuously elaborated technology to meet those needs. The desolation of Parys Mountain in Anglesey, an example of the complete destruction about 1800 of a natural environment in the exploitation of what was considered the world's largest known resource of copper, illustrates the impact of the Industrial Revolution upon the landscape. The same theme of the total transformation of a landscape by industry and its subsequent dereliction is treated in the pages that describe the lower Swansea valley and, as the studies of the Bedfordshire claypits and the china-clay workings of St Austell reveal, the extinction of the countryside and its resources by the hungry demands of a single industry remains with us on an even grander scale in the twentieth century.

Man's relationship to Nature has not been one only of destruction and exploitation. Perhaps the most abiding feature of British landscapes is a continuing relationship between societies and their environment. Relict objects in the countryside from each succeeding phase of Britain's history colour her regions and localities today. The topics illustrated in the following pages deal with a limited but contrasted selection of surviving features — prehistoric stone circles, churches, field systems — from the different stages of history. Our landscapes have often been described as a palimpsest, a comparison with medieval parchment that might be used several times over to preserve writing of differing dates and kind. The palimpsest of the British landscape harks back to prehistory. Some of the oldest and grandest objects that have survived to the present day are the stone circles of late Neolithic- and Bronze-Age origin. Stonehenge in Wiltshire and Callanish in the Hebrides, far removed from each other in distance, contain the same

mysteries and point to the same kind of prehistoric society. They were raised by a people with a considerable knowledge of astronomy, mathematics and practical technology in the laying out of monuments composed of standing stones each of which weighed several tons. The location, too, of the greatest stone circles suggests a regional organisation of economy and society some 4,000 years ago. Stonehenge in its position on the chalk plateau of Salisbury Plain seems to indicate a regional node in the human geography of southern Britain. Further north, in the Peak District, a simpler monument from the same period, Arbor Low, suggests a focal point in the Carboniferous Limestone plateau of the High Peak — a region of rich soils confined within the bleak rim of high gritstone moorlands of which the Roaches forms a part.

The most formative of the early stages of British landscape history occupies the centuries between the incursion of the first Iron-Age settlers about 500BC and the beginning of the Anglo-Saxon colonisation in the fifth century AD. During this span of almost a thousand years a mature Celtic civilisation determined the outlines of so many landscape features that have survived, although dimly or else changed out of all recognition. To these times we owe the earliest stratum of our place-names. In eastern and southern England the relics of the British epoch among surviving place-names are indeed sparse, but to the north west in highland Britain a direct link with the culture of the Celtic Iron Age was retained as the societies of Wales, Scotland and Cornwall evolved through the post-Roman centuries. The most lasting and striking Iron-Age relics are the ramparted and ditch-encircled enclosures that crown so many hill-tops and narrow spurs up and down our islands. A large number of these camps, such as the scarcely investigated sites on the summits of the Clwydian Hills in North Wales, seemed to have no connection with the evolution of society in Britain after the Romans. They appeared to be stranded elements — fossils in the landscape — of a culture and society that was obliterated by the Saxon invasions and settlements. Lately research in archaeology and historical geography has taken a fresh view of these impressive and mysterious earthworks. Close investigation at a handful of 'forts' such as Cadbury Camp in Somerset and The Breidden among the wooded hills of the Welsh Marches has shown that they were inhabited long after the abandonment of these islands by the Romans. In addition there is much fresh evidence that some of the forts were inhabited at an early date, even before the end of the Bronze Age. The length of occupation of some of our Iron-Age camps may therefore stretch to more than a thousand years and in that time certain sites have contained communities of several hundred people whose functions included craft industries, trade and the practice of religion. The sites of some of our important towns may be closely connected with places that were already important in the organisation of Iron-Age Britain. The Romans established towns at Canterbury and Dorchester among a host of other places close beside existing Iron-Age earthworks; Shrewsbury was probably founded within the core of a hill-fort encircled by the Severn and there is a hint that Edinburgh castle, the focus of the old town, was built over the site of a prehistoric earthwork.

History read through the features of a landscape takes on different dimensions and relationships from history read in textbooks. The Britain of the Romans or the Saxon kingdoms of Northumbria and Mercia is overlaid by all that has happened since in the way of political history. The landscape still preserves features of these long forgotten territories, none perhaps more impressive than the frontier-works that were raised in attempts to define their political boundaries — Offa's Dyke, the western boundary of Mercia towards the close of the eighth century, and the Roman Wall that for a time served as the north-western limit of a world empire as well as defining the frontier of a political unit based on lowland England.

The expansion of cities and the spread of urban conurbations since the last quarter of the nineteenth century have been offset by efforts to preserve relics of older and vanishing landscapes. The making of National Parks, discussed under the Brecon Beacons, is one aspect of this movement. But the need for landscape conservation concerns more than the preservation of tracts of great natural beauty. Wicken Fen in Cambridgeshire is a relic of a man-made medieval landscape that in its turn was swept away by the great reclamation of the Fenland that began in the seventeenth century. But it now seems necessary to preserve a fragment of a medieval man-made landscape that has survived almost by accident. The conservationists of these latter decades of the twentieth century feel an increasing need to preserve tracts of wilderness in the remotest parts of highland Britain. The Cuillins of western Skye, as untouched by man as any part of these islands, must be left as a reserve for the mountaineer and rock climber. The creation of the Beinn Eighe Nature Reserve marks off a tract of the north-west Highlands where the threats to the wilderness may seem slight at the present time.

Each object of the landscape — towns and their streets and buildings, roads and fields and hedgerows — can be analysed in the terms of its history. The regions of Britain and their intimate local variations as we see them today have evolved through two time scales, the immensely long span of geological time and the far shorter one of human pre-history and recorded history in which Man himself has taken over an increasingly important role as the maker of our landscape.

Stac Polly, Ross and Cromarty: residual mountains

Isolated and dominating the grassy shores of Loch Lurgain, Stac Polly has now lost its quartzite capping but still retains its residual appearance

Suilven, a near neighbour of Stac Polly presents a blunt nose at the western end of the sandstone ridge which makes up the greater part of the mountain. Here the protective capping of hard quartzite has survived

For all its summer invasion by motorists and caravans, the north-west Highlands remains one of the great empty spaces of Britain. It is also one of the most fascinating, for its various rock types have given rise to a distinctive suite of landforms. The hard, uncompromising Lewisian Gneiss tends to form low plateau country deeply scored and bared by the recent passage of ice, a country where land and water seem to be in equal proportion. Rising out of this loch-studded landscape are isolated mountains, each a self-contained unit though mainly of elongated form.

All are developed out of the Torridonian Sandstone formation, a rich plum-red colour on a sunlit day and showing prominent bedding planes. It is the sandstone, above all else, which gives this province of Assynt its imaginative and distinctive setting. The rock is hard enough to give rise to steep slopes but always offers opportunity for

erosion to carve it into curious shapes.

The lone ridge of Stac Polly (Pollaidh in Gaelic) shows the effects well. It rises to just over 2,000ft (608m) near its western end and is seen to advantage from the shores of Loch Lurgain to the south. Its slopes look steep and forbidding from below though it is possible to scramble up the screes to reach the summit ridge without too much difficulty. Along the top the sandstone has weathered into a series of pinnacles, too small to effectively determine the shape of the mountain as a whole but serving as a reminder that erosion is taking place continuously with the object of removing the mountain altogether. Stac Polly has already suffered more in this respect than its near neighbours a few miles away across the gneiss country to the north. These two mountains, Suilven and Canisp, are similar to Stac Polly in that they form isolated ridges of sandstone rising well above the plateau surface. Surmounting the sandstone, however, is a capping of hard grey quartzite rock which affords greater protection to the softer beds beneath. Stac Polly once had its quartzite too, but lost it as part of the ever-continuing process of landscape reduction. As yet, the mountain still retains the basic form of a narrow ridge which it had when its quartzite capping was still in place.

Further reading: Murray, W. H. *The Companion Guide to the West Highlands of Scotland* (Collins, 1973)

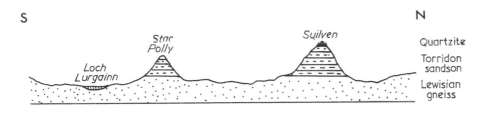

Between the isolated mountains the terrain is plateau-like and deeply scoured by ice which has left behind a cluster of tiny lochans in the over-deepened hollows in the Lewisian Gneiss

A cross-section showing the residual mountains rising out of the gneiss plateau

Pre-Cambrian island: Charnwood Forest, Leicestershire

that the features which make up an exciting landscape are lacking.

Charnwood Forest, lying close to the city of Leicester on its north-west side, is the exception to this broad generalisation. The reason why Charnwood stands out as a distinctive enclave lies in the fact that over a few square miles the old, hard basement rocks of Pre-Cambrian age — some of the oldest in the country — project through the more recent cover of clays, marls and sandstones. Ancient volcanoes, perhaps dating back some 700 million years, threw out a variety of material which was later compacted and crushed to form the hard, resistant rocks which dominate the Charnwood scene. In addition there is a whole succession of crystalline rocks which have been extensively quarried at places like Groby and Mountsorrel.

With nearly all the complex rock types resisting erosion it is not surprising that bare crags are such a feature of Charnwood. They occur both in the gorge-like valleys like the one running through Bradgate Park and also on the ridge tops at Beacon Hill and High Sharpley. In the latter situation they project well above the general surface level and more than one observer has likened them to the tors of Dartmoor. They are less regular in appearance, however, and at High Sharpley they stand up almost vertical like the spine of some prehistoric monster. The rocky eminences undoubtedly suffered from the severe effects of weathering during the Ice Age particularly when Charnwood Forest stood out above the sea of ice all around. Not all of Charnwood has this rocky appearance for the valleys often have an infill of much younger rocks which give an altogether softer scene. Occasionally in some of the old slate quarries around Swithland this younger sandstone can be seen left in hollows cut in the much harder rock. We are now witnessing the slow but gradual uncovering of the ancient landscape which developed on the Pre-Cambrian rocks in the distant past.

Many of the hilltops of Charnwood Forest are crowned with bare rock outcrops which resemble the tors of Dartmoor. Some like this group at High Sharpley have a splintery appearance, possibly due to frost shattering in the closing stages of the Ice Age

Few would regard the landscape of the East Midlands as exciting and yet in spite of its lack of appeal to those in search of the dramatic, it is a pleasant unspoiled countryside of hedged fields, of quiet lanes with broad verges and a scattering of planted copses. Nearly everywhere there are soft rocks which yield easily to the forces of erosion so

The gorge in Bradgate Park was formed as the tiny Linford Brook breached the hard rock edge to the Forest in making its way to the softer marl country surrounding it. Formerly a medieval deer park, Bradgate abounds in pollarded oak and more recently planted conifers

Another ancient rock found here is the Swithland Slate which was formerly quarried in small pits. Most of these are now flooded and their margins overgrown. The Swithland slate was extensively used as a local roofing material prior to the introduction of the thinner Welsh variety

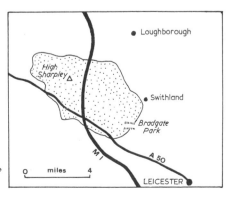

Charnwood Forest lying north-west of Leicester

Further reading: Pye, N. (ed). *Leicester and its Region* (Leicester University Press, 1972)

A mountain in history: Snowdon, Gwynedd

The contrasting slopes of the Clogau ridge leading to the distant summit of Snowdon. To the left the land falls abruptly to the Llanberis Pass. Its steep, craggy, ice-shorn slopes contrast sharply with the more gentle topography falling away to the right. The mountain railway hugs this smooth slope as it climbs to the summit

From almost every viewpoint Snowdon has the appearance of a mountain, and although its exact height of 3,506ft (1,066m) was not determined until early nineteenth-century tradition had linked the mountain with being the highest peak of the whole range.

Lying in an isolated corner of north-west Wales, where Welsh national aspirations lasted well into the Middle Ages, its English name is of long standing. In the *Anglo-Saxon Chronicle* it is recorded that in 1095 William Rufus came north with his armies to 'Snawdun'. The name persisted and with it the tradition that here was a region of high mountains permanently covered with snow. Camden, as late as 1586, perpetuated this myth in his great topographical account of the whole kingdom; for while snow patches often last on the mountain until early June,

none survive the heat of the summer sun. With the increasing interest in topography and map-making which began to make itself felt towards the end of the sixteenth century, the isolation of the area was gradually broken down and more realistic views were expressed. Even so, the cartographer, John Speed, who produced a series of county maps of England and Wales together with descriptive notes in 1610, went as far as suggesting that 'these mountains may not unfitly be called the British Alps and for their steepness and cragginess not unlike those of Italy'.

In 1781 the traveller Thomas Pennant published his *Journey to Snowdon*, which gave a much truer perspective. He ascended Snowdon by several different routes and could really lay claim to being the first true mountaineer of the area. He was also acutely aware of the

16

natural scenery, as his descriptive writing clearly shows. On one occasion he spent the night on the summit of Snowdon in order to see the sunrise. The publication of Pennant's book started a fashion for exploring the wilder parts of the country, often in search of the horrific and awe-inspiring as well as the picturesque beauty which only mountain scenery could provide. But soon pressure of numbers was beginning to make itself felt so that when George Borrow, author of *Wild Wales*, came to Snowdon in the 1850s he found it thronged with groups of people. By the end of the century a rack and pinion railway had reached the summit and with it the last vestige of remoteness disappeared for all time.

Further Reading: Condry, W. *Snowdonia National Park* (Collins, 1966)

The twin corrie basins of Glaslyn (upper) and Llyn Llydaw (lower) around the edge of which the Pyg track makes for the summit

One of the classic views of the Snowdon range taken from near Capel Curig across the water of Llynnau Mymbyr

Granite and gabbro topography: the Cuillin Hills, Skye

The island of Skye in the Inner Hebrides has two distinct parts. In the south there is the mountain knot of the rugged Cuillin Hills, which at their highest reach 3,257ft (992m) on Sgurr Alasdair. To the north lie the peninsular extensions where the landscape is dominated by flat-topped plateaux, often descending in a series of steps to the coast. This basic contrast is a reflection of the two main types of rock which make up the island. The northern part of the island of Skye is made up of a succession of lava flows, whereas the Cuillins are fashioned out of the igneous rocks of gabbro and granite. Both groups of rocks have come from the bowels of the earth but, whereas the gabbro and granite cooled slowly at depth, the lavas were outpoured at the surface from volcanoes which were active some 50 million years ago. The best view of the contrasting areas of the Cuillins is from within and can readily be seen by taking the track which leads up Glen Sligachan, an effective divide between the granite and gabbro mountains.

The central core of the Black Cuillins looking northward towards the twin peaks of Am Bhasteir and Sgurr nan Gillean. The gabbro has been heavily scored by passing ice but it provides good holds for the climber

Loch Coruisk has been hollowed out by ice to well below sea level even though it is but a short distance inland

18

Glamaig, in the Red Hills, as seen across the Sound of Raasay with the jagged peaks of the Black Cuillins beyond. In the foreground a raised beach provides good farmland

Gabbro scenery

Within the Cuillins, even, there are differences in scenery which arise from the way in which the gabbro and granite have reacted to the forces of weathering and erosion. Gabbro is a hard, compacted rock which defies erosion, even though it has been subject to intense abrasion and scraping by ice as recently as 10,000 years ago. The country to which it gives rise, known as the Black Cuillins because of the dull-grey colouring of its rocks and general forbidding appearance, is wild and inaccessible save for climbers who cherish its difficult slopes. There are almost twenty peaks which top the 3,000ft (900m) contour, arranged in a ring around the deeply set Loch Coruisk Running through the gabbro are narrow dykes of a more brittle rock and where these have been removed the ridge crest develops upstanding pinnacles as part of a serrated skyline.

Granite scenery

The neighbouring Red Hills of Skye are fashioned out of granite. Granite reacts very differently from gabbro to the forces of erosion and as a result the hill summits are more rounded and great screes of debris form a prominent apron at their foot. Shades of pink and light-grey give mountains like Glamaig, Marsco and Beinn na Caillich a much warmer appearance than those farther west — the peaks of the Black Cuillins.

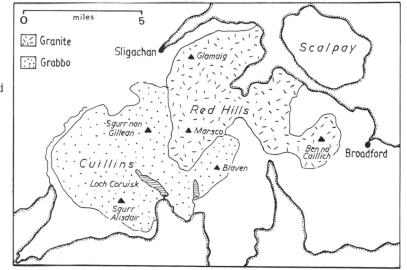

Both the granite and gabbro areas suffered intense erosion during the Ice Age and the detailed fashioning of each dates from this time. Great corrie basins were hollowed out and steep knife-edged ridges developed in both rock types.

Distribution of the gabbro and granite areas in the Cuillins and Red Hills

Further reading: Murray, W. H. *The Islands of Western Scotland* (Eyre Methuen, 1973)

19

England's highest mountain: Scafell Pike, Cumbria

The twin peaks of Scafell and Scafell Pike separated by the gash of Mickledore where a weaker dyke rock has suffered erosion to form a high-level col between the two mountain tops

The central massif of the Lake District with its assemblage of high peaks, is the roof of England. Here there is a knot which ties together a number of convergent ridges, each impressive in its own right and with its own distinctive features which lend diversity to the whole. The Scafell ridge has four pikes or peaks, of which Scafell Pike is the highest at 3,210ft (975m).

Its volcanic rocks, hardened through time to form green slates, have responded to the attacks of frost and ice and in places give rise to great precipices, bare crags and a knobbly terrain which speaks defiance at the natural forces intent on destruction. The whole ridge, beginning in the impressive wall of Great End in the north and ending in Slight Side with

its bare crags overlooking Upper Eskdale, has much to offer both to the ordinary fell walker and the serious climber. In Broad Stand, first climbed by Coleridge, and the nearby rock faces, there are some of the most arduous and difficult ascents of the whole Lake District. The ridge between the two peaks of Scafell Pike and the slightly lower but in many ways more impressive Scafell — lying to the south — is broken by the gap of Mickledore, etched out as erosion has successfully attacked a dyke of weakened rock. From the summit cairn on the Pike the aspect is of mountains not of lakes. On a clear day, when a north-wester is bringing in polar air, the view takes in the nearby Great Gable and Pillar while away to the north-east,

The main Scafell range as seen from Hardknott Fell across the valley of Upper Eskdale. This country was a great sheep range for the monks of Furness Abbey who established their grange farms in the area

Each view of Scafell gives the mountain a different appearance as is clear from this outline seen from the shores of Wastwater

in the middle distance, Skiddaw and Saddleback are visible. Distant views on days of exceptional visibility include the distinctive outlines of the Isle of Man, and the hills of Galloway, while to the south the Carnedds in North Wales may sometimes be seen. Even Slieve Dionard in Ireland is not beyond bounds and its appearance recalls the efforts of the Ordnance Survey in its early days when it used both mountains to establish a link between the surveys of England and Ireland.

The entire summit is under the guardianship of the National Trust. Scafell Pike was given by Lord Leconsfield in 1919 as a memorial to the men of Cumbria who died in World War I. Scafell was also given to the Trust and with it a thousand or more acres above the 2,000ft (600m) contour. In spite of the litter left behind by the thousands who climb England's highest peak, its acquisition by the Trust will ensure that future generations will be able to enjoy the fine panorama of views from its top.

Further reading: Millward, R. and Robinson, A. H. W. *The Lake District* (Eyre Methuen, 1970)

Granite tors: Dartmoor, Devon

Seen from within or even afar, the Dartmoor countryside is mainly one of gentle, rounded slopes with flat-topped ridges rising out of wide, open valleys. Many of the tops are crowned with upstanding rock masses, the tors. Why should these hard core remnants survive when the granite all around seems to have disintegrated under the attacks of weathering?

If a tor is studied at close hand, it will be seen to be split into blocks by gaps or joints which can run either vertically or horizontally. The vertical joints are particularly important in that they allow the surface rain-water to penetrate into the granite and there begin the task of rotting away the rock. The whole process is slow acting at present, but in the tors of today we see the work, only half completed. Tors are simply big blocks of granite which have so far resisted complete reduction. It would seem that the spacing of the joints is an important factor for where they are wide apart the tor stands a much better chance of survival. Where the joints run close together the whole of the granite may rot away to a considerable depth and no tor will form.

Granite as a rock has a reputation for toughness and durability and has therefore been used widely in building harbour works and other defences

Comberstone Tor overlooking the open Dart valley near Dartmeet. The granite has weathered along false horizontal bedding planes and many blocks have been prised from the main outcrop and litter the slopes around

Haytor Rocks form perhaps the most visited group of tors on Dartmoor for they are accessible from the Bovey Tracey to Dartmeet road. Haytor shows both vertical and horizontal lines of weakness along which weathering takes place

against the sea. When a freshly broken piece of granite is examined it can be seen to consist of three main minerals: quartz, a grey translucent material; felspar with its long white crystals; and thin flakes of brown mica which make the rock glisten in bright sunlight. Despite its apparent toughness, the granite will weather when attacked by rain and frost and ultimately will completely disintegrate. When this happens the felspar forms a soft whitish clay while the insoluble residue of quartz crystals forms a gritty sand known as growan. This breakdown of the rock is of great importance in any understanding of the origin and form of the Dartmoor landscape.

Tors are hardly evolving under present-day conditions. Their greatest period of development would seem to have been during the extreme climatic conditions of the Ice Age when the area was subject to intense frost action. This would lead to a prising away of the granite from the sides of the tor, forming the apron of rock fragments or clitter which surrounds the rocky eminences in many parts of present-day Dartmoor.

Further reading: Millward, R. and Robinson, A. H. W. *The South West Peninsula* (Macmillan, 1971)

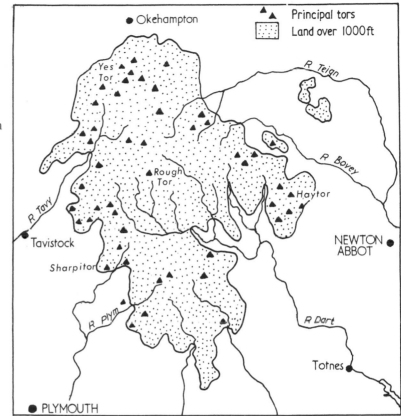

Location of the principal tors on Dartmoor

Granite was a much-prized building stone in the last century and this 'railway' with its granite track was laid down to tap the Haytor quarry

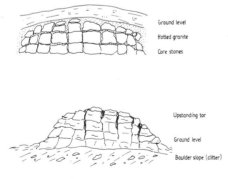

Tor formation by sub-surface rotting of the granite

National Park scenery: Brecon Beacons, South Wales

The Brecon Beacons National Park forms one of the least spoiled tracts of country in south Wales in spite of its lying cheek by jowl with the disfigured landscape of the coalfield to the south. Within its boundaries there is a rich variety of scenery with the thick, dark sandstone beds making the most forceful impression.

At their highest point, Pen y Fan, a few miles south of Brecon, the Beacons approach within a 100ft (30m) of the 3,000ft (900m) contour. Here the area is bare moorland, ideal as upland pasture for sheep from the farms down in the valley. Although the whole area is thinly populated, its magnificent scenery is the delight of thousands who visit the National Park each year. It has yet to experience the tourist traffic to which the Lake District and Peak National Parks have been subjected in recent years. To many its relative unpopularity is its principal attraction.

The sharp cornice marking the top of the north-facing scarp of the main Brecon Beacon range. A capping of hard sandstone and conglomerate protects the softer beds below from erosion. Hard bands occur throughout the upper-most beds and often stand out distinctively

Blaen y Glyn waterfall near the head of the Talybont valley where a small stream encounters a harder sandstone bed. Behind rises the prominent scarp edge around Cwar y Gigfran

24

Formation

Snow and ice collected here at various times during the Ice Age when the present cwm-like form of the valleys running down to the Usk were formed. The rock formations are everywhere dipping to the south with the result that there is a magnificent escarpment of sandstone facing north over the Usk valley. Along its crest is a sharp cornice which grades into the top of the steep backslope that heads each of the small valleys.

Some of these cwms contain small lakes held up by dumps of morainic debris. The ice which collected along the scarp face obviously acted as a chisel and gouged out this impressive succession of deep hollows which give a scalloped margin to the crest line of the Beacons. On top, however, the scenery changes as the backslope is followed down towards the valleys of the coalfield. Here the ice has acted more like a smoothing-plane, giving rounded tops and gentle interfluves.

History

The concept of a National Park as an area whose natural beauty would be safeguarded for future generations to enjoy is of long standing. Wordsworth was perhaps the first to appreciate the virtues of conservation in his beloved Lakeland when he wrote of it as a national property 'in which every man has a right and interest who has an eye to perceive and a heart to enjoy'. He anticipated events by more than a century, for it was 1950 before our first National Park became a reality.

The Brecon Beacons Park, covering over 500 square miles (1,294 sq km), was designated in 1957.

Further reading: Davies, M. (ed). *Brecon Beacons National Park* (H.M.S.O., 1967)

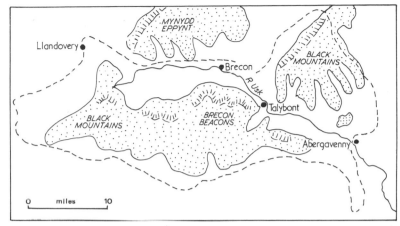

The extent of the Brecon Beacons National Park

The line of the Brecon Beacons scarp with its deeply scoured combes on its northern side

Volcanic hills: the Sidlaws, Angus

The Midland Valley or Central Lowlands of Scotland, sandwiched between two sets of faults, is something of a misnomer for within it is a number of pronounced hill ranges which even exceed 2,000ft (608m) in places. Each is formed of volcanic rocks which resist erosion much more effectively than the sandstones around them. Each rises abruptly out of the plains and, because they carry a very different vegetation from the rich lowland farms, they form islands of moor or hill pastures, once despised, but now of great value as open spaces in this leisure-conscious age.

The Sidlaws are typical of these volcanic islands which straddle the Midland Valley in a general south-west to north-east direction. Their unity is geological rather than topographical for the hills are very much broken by transverse valleys running across them from Strathmore to the carse lands bordering on the Firth of Tay. The succession of lava flows which make up the hills is of ancient date and, layer upon layer, were outpoured over a long period of time. The lava beds dip to the north where they pass under the sandstone lowlands of Strathmore. To the south they present a steep scarp slope overlooking the country behind Dundee. The effects of past vulcanism are not restricted to the Sidlaw Hills, Dundee Law (571ft, 174m), within the city, is a prominent hill marking the site of an old volcanic vent. Its striking appearance is in contrast to the gentle country bordering on the Tay, the Carse of Gowrie, with its fertile soils derived from the rich estuarine clays.

With the adjacent rich farmlands of the Carse of Gowrie and Strathmore on their flanks, the Sidlaw Hills form a negative area mainly under moorland and hill pasture with the occasional conifer plantation to provide some diversity. Numerous small lochs occur, especially in the central section, and some of these have been turned into reservoirs to supply the Tayside towns. Like so many uplands which rise abruptly out of well-farmed lowlands,

the attraction of the Sidlaws lies in the open country on top, and the view it provides, especially of the distant Grampians away to the north. Although the Sidlaws are not as high as the neighbouring Ochils between Perth and Stirling they reach 1,236ft (376m) at King's Seat and rise to 1,492ft (456m) on Craigow Hill, a few miles north of Dundee.

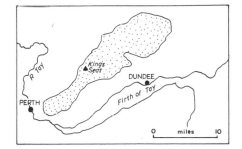

Further reading: Sissons, J. *The Evolution of Scotland's Scenery* (Oliver & Boyd, 1967)

Due to the dip of the volcanic beds to the north, the Sidlaws present their steepest face to the south where they overlook the rich carse lands bordering on the Firth of Tay

Sidlaw Hills between Perth and Dundee

(opposite) **Kinnoull Hill, an outlier of the main ridge of the Sidlaws which overlooks the city of Perth from the east. On its summit an eighteenth century castle recalls the age when it was fashionable to imitate, in this case a French chateau**

Limestone escarpment: Eglwyseg Rocks, Clwyd

Eglwyseg or Church Rocks, named from the nearby Valle Crucis Abbey, has a stepped appearance due to a succession of harder limestone bands within the whole formation. The lower slope is formed of loose scree, a jumble of boulders through which vegetation attempts to maintain a precarious hold

The traveller using Thomas Telford's Holyhead Road, the present A5, is presented with a complete change of scene once he crosses the Welsh border at Chirk. The low rolling landscape of Shropshire gives way to the foothills of the Welsh mountains. Only the river valleys like the Vale of Llangollen form strips of lowland and even here the hillsides crowd in on every side. Along the northern edge the scenery is dominated by the bare scars of limestone forming the Eglwyseg Rocks. This is impressive at a distance though rather

overpowering at close hand.

The escarpment consists of a sequence of hard limestone beds with thin bands of shale in between. Initially the scarp face must have been considerably steeper, but weathering of its upper shoulder and the building of a scree of loose boulders at its foot have softened its outline. Much of the weathering took place during the Ice Age when frost shattering went on unimpeded; At the same time, gully erosion was etching out deep salients into the scarp face to give it a scalloped

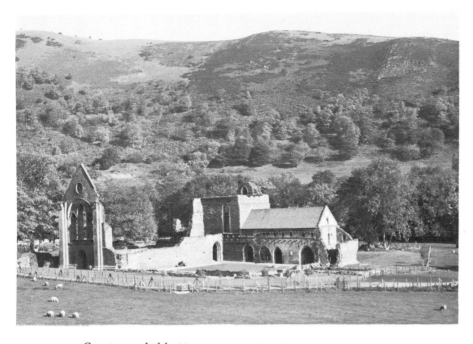

Valle Crucis Abbey was formerly a monastery, founded in 1189 amidst the lush pastures of the valley floor with the Eglwyseg edge forming a backcloth

Castell Dinas Bran, set on an isolated hill in front of the main limestone scarp, has long been a favoured defensive site for there are remains ranging in age from the Iron Age right through to medieval times on the hill summit

appearance. Great rounded buttresses now thrust forward at intervals, clearly ripe for attack should glacial conditions ever return to the area. The line of the Eglwyseg scarp coincides with a major fault which has the effect of bringing together two very dissimilar rock types, each offering varying degrees of resistance to erosion. Standing out in front of the scarp is the hill of Dinas Bran. This is formed of shale which, although it resists erosion, is nothing like as effective scenically as the limestone. The hill of Dinas Bran nevertheless forms a prominent landmark especially when seen from the town of Llangollen below.

Because of its isolation and all-round view, Dinas Bran was fortified during the Dark Ages and there are still masonry remains on its summit. The name Eglwyseg probably refers to the fact that the escarpment was at that time under the ownership of the Cistercian abbey of Valle Crucis, founded in 1201 and only a short distance away in a side valley of the Dee.

Further reading: Millward, R. and Robinson, A. H. W. *The Welsh Marches* (Macmillan, 1971)

A major fault is responsible for the cliff of Gordale Scar where a small stream tumbles over the edge in a series of falls from the limestone plateau above

(opposite) Beyond the limestone cliff the plateau stretches away to the north with Malham Tarn in the middle distance. Deep incisions at Gordale Scar and Malham Cove (extreme left) are spectacular features which owe their origin to more active surface streams at the close of the Ice Age

Limestone erosion

Limestone as a rock has special characteristics which in turn are reflected in the landscape with which it is closely associated. It is a rock of great hardness and durability — hence its extensive use as road metal — and yet it is pervious, swallowing up water like a sponge. The reason lies in the extensive system of vertical joints and pronounced bedding planes. Water which is slightly acid through dissolving carbon dioxide of the atmosphere can dissolve the surface coating of the limestone. In this way it gradually widens the joints and

opens up horizontal passages along the bedding planes. Over a period of time the whole surface drainage passes underground where sizeable streams burrow through an intricate network of channels, often opening out into huge caverns. The stream will only re-emerge at the surface where it encounters an underlying impervious bed which prevents its further downward passage.

The country around Malham in Craven at the head of Airedale has a rich assemblage of landforms which owe their origin and detailed form to the thick beds of mountain limestone which outcrop in this central part of the

30

Pennines. North of the village is Malham Cove, a great amphitheatre enclosed by a rock wall almost 300ft (90m) high. At its foot there is a keld or spring, to feed Malham Beck which ultimately goes to swell the waters of the river Aire. On the plateau top above there are extensive areas of bare limestone where the vertical joints have been widened to form 'grykes'. Much of the limestone pavement is without soil or vegetation but ferns and other damp-loving plants often grow within the grykes. The area of the plateau top is waterless country though the presence of narrow, dry valleys show that this was not always the case. In the Ice Age, for example, surface flow must have been considerable and water would then have poured over the steep backwall of Malham Cove.

Gordale Scar

A mile to the east of the cove the long line of the limestone cliff is broken by a narrow rift down which a waterfall tumbles from a hole high up the rock face. This is Gordale Scar and it is possible to scramble up the side of the fall on to the plateau top. The valley above, unlike at Malham, contains water, for it is plenteously supplied from a rather marshy area of clay a mile farther upstream. Gordale Beck is one of the few streams which manage to flow on the top of the limestone plateau.

Further reading: Raistrick, A. *The Pennine Dales* (Eyre & S., 1968)

Limestone features around Malham

Gritstone country: the Roaches, Staffordshire

Along its western edge the tough gritstone beds present an imposing face to the lowland pastures of rural Staffordshire

Ramshaw Rocks along the eastern margin of the Roaches has weathered to give a series of curiously shaped rocks seen by every traveller taking the main Leek to Buxton road

The name Roaches simply means rocks and this adequately sums up the character of this small tract of country on the western fringes of the Peak District. It is not known with certainty when the name was first given, though as a corruption of the French *roches* it may date from Norman times.

The various rocks all belong to the Millstone Grit formation with a small overlay of Coal Measure strata in the centre of the area. They form an alternating sequence of hard grit layers with intervening shale bands. The grits give rise to rocky ridges while the softer shales coincide with valleys or lowlands. Much of the distinctive character of the area has arisen through the folding of the various rock formations. Broadly speaking the Roaches consist of a sharp syncline or downfold, rather like a pie dish with the tough gritstone formations forming the rim. In the centre of the dish is the low-lying and ill-drained Goldsitch Moss where the

Coal Measures are exposed. Although mainly shales they include a few thin seams of coal which were once worked in small bell-pits. The rather dull landscape of this tiny coalfield has the effect of giving greater emphasis to the surrounding rock ridges. To the east lie the Ramshaw Rocks, which must have been a familiar landmark to the Roman legions who tramped the road en route for Buxton. The bare rocky spine is not of great length, but due to the sharp dip of the beds, it thrusts out eastwards, often overhanging the boulder slope below. On the other side of the downfold there is a similar ridge of bare rock, the Roaches proper. Here the dip of the beds towards the centre of the basin makes them jut out in a westward direction. Many of the rocks have been carved into curious shapes by the action of wind, rain and frost which bite deeply into their weaker parts.

Hen Cloud

A drop into a col at the southern end of the Roaches ridge is followed by a climb up to the top of the isolated Hen Cloud, perhaps the most impressive single feature of the entire area. Although the whole area is privately owned, access is now allowed along the path which follows the ridge top. The steep western face is much favoured as a nursery slope for climbers anxious to learn the basic techniques before venturing to more difficult areas like the Lake District and Snowdonia.

Further reading: Millward, R. and Robinson, A. H. W. *The Peak District* (Eyre Methuen, 1975)

The pie dish effect of the Roaches

Hen Cloud, the southern bastion of the Roaches is perhaps the most impressive landform of the whole group

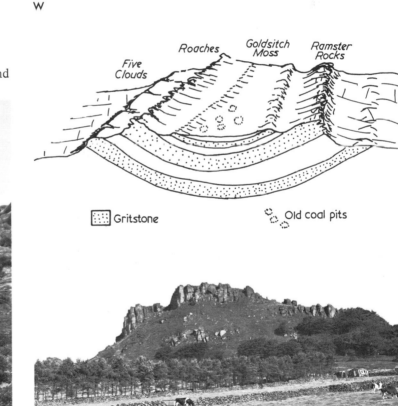

W   E

Five Clouds   Roaches   Goldsitch Moss   Ramster Rocks

▒ Gritstone   ⭕ Old coal pits

Chalk cliffline: Seven Sisters, Sussex

The sea-eroded face of the rolling landscape of the Sussex downland with its sharply truncated ridge and valley succession

The line of white cliffs which stretches from the North Foreland right through to the Devon-Dorset boundary represents perhaps the most typical of English coastal settings. Both invaders and traders from prehistoric times onwards must have become very familiar with its appearance as they crossed the narrow divide from the continent and relied on it for identifiable landmarks in the days before navigation became an exact science. One of the most distinctive cliff outlines occurs in the section running eastwards from the mouth of the Cuckmere river as far as Birling Gap, close to Beachy Head. A succession of shorn-off ridges and valleys has given rise to an undulating cliff top for long known as the Seven Sisters. The wavy outline of the Seven Sisters cliffs is a direct result of the way in which the sea has attacked the chalk downland country behind.

In common with other parts of the South Downs, the chalk landscape is a waterless country made up of a succession of wide-open valleys and broad exposed ridge tops. Although steep slopes occur in places, especially along the scarp crest in the north where it overlooks the wooded acres of the Weald, for the most part it is a rolling countryside of soft outlines and gentle swells. The ability of the chalk to 'swallow' surface water has meant that although the rock is relatively soft, the downland is an area of fairly hilly relief. Valleys which once contained water are now dry and are not being lowered to any great extent under present conditions.

Along the coastline, however, conditions are very different. The sea is actively cutting back the chalk cliffs at quite a rapid rate. Measurements of cliff-top recession at Birling Gap have shown that it can reach as much as 1m a year on average. The greatest erosion occurs during the winter months when both marine attack and ordinary weathering processes are more effective. During a severe winter the soft chalk of the cliffs readily succumbs to frost shattering and cliff falls are common. It is only at this time that the cliff face takes on a sparkling white appearance; at other times it is a dull grey in colour. As the sea, rain, and frost bite deeply into the bare, exposed edge of the downland surface, so the valleys have been left high and dry, so that today they hang well above the level of the shore.

Further reading: Millward, R. and Robinson, A. H. W. *South-East England: The Channel Coastlands* (Macmillan, 1973)

The Seven Sisters as viewed from the east at Birling Gap

The hanging valley to the west of the Cuckmere river with its floor partially infilled with more recent sediments, the product of mass movement of debris down the valley slopes during the Ice Age

Inland the chalk downland ends abruptly in the north-facing scarp which looks out over the wooded landscape of the Sussex Weald

35

Ice-Age valley: Louth, Lincolnshire

The breach made in the long
chalk spur between Fisher's
and Hubbard's Hill near
Louth as a result of ice
interference. The steep sides
to the gap are clothed in
beechwoods

The six long barrows on
Orgath Hill near Louth, a
reminder that early man
found the Wolds landscape
attractive after the end of the
Ice Age. One of his prehistoric
tracks, the Bluestone Road, is
named from the distinctive
glacial erratics found in the
glacial clays left behind by
the ice

Although the action of ice in shaping the landscape is most clearly seen in the more mountainous parts of Britain, it was also effective in lowland areas, though acting in a more subtle fashion. The Lincolnshire Wolds, a great belt of chalk downland extending from the fenny margins of the Wash to the Humber shores, shows how ice could create an entirely new pattern of drainage over limited areas. Because of the dip of the chalk beds, the Wolds present a bold scarp to the west and a more gentle dip slope running down to the marshland strip bordering on the coast. This dip slope is broken by a series of parallel valleys, now mainly dry except in their lower parts. In between the valleys there are long spurs of chalk. Occasionally these are severed by clean gashes cut right across them. One such gap — now the site of a public park — occurs about a mile to the west of the market town of Louth. A small stream flows through the gap between Fisher's and Hubbard's Hill and in doing so it forsakes any obvious, more direct course towards the coast by turning through a right angle. The gap is best seen from the A153 road about a mile south-west of Louth. It can be examined at close hand by walking through the park from one end to the other. The sides of the channel are cut entirely in chalk and are especially steep in the cliff under Hubbard's Hill.

The reason for this anomalous course of the stream, repeated elsewhere in the Lincolnshire Wolds, lies in the events which took place in the closing stages of the Ice Age. Then, about 20,000 years ago, a great ice mass moved down the East Coast, extending only a short distance inland. Its inner edge lay along the lower fringe of the chalk dip slope, the upper parts of the Wolds being free from ice. During warm interludes when stream flow was possible, water cut a series of channels along the ice margin, in many cases running completely across spurs like the one at Fisher's Hill. When the ice finally melted away the gash was sufficiently deep for it to be

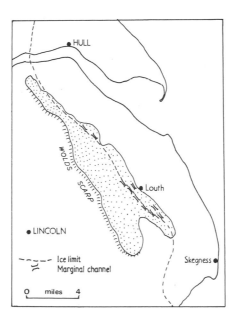

The limits of ice penetration in Lincolnshire and the associated features

The Wolds proved attractive in later centuries as great sheep-rearing areas and in some cases this conversion to pastures led to the abandonment of villages like Calceby whose crumbling church is now the only tangible evidence of a former flourishing settlement

used by the stream as the main valley rather than resume its original, more direct, course towards the sea. In this way, as a consequence of ice interference, this transverse element in the drainage pattern came into being.

Further reading: Robinson, A. H. W. and Wallwork, K. L. *Map Studies and Field Excursions* (Longman, 1971)

Louth, which serves as the main market town for this part of the Wolds, retains its quiet Georgian streets which surround the impressive fifteenth century church

Cumbrian lake: Ullswater

lower reach of the lake extends as far as Pooley Bridge. The isolated hill of Dunmallet, with its wooded slopes and top crowned with an Iron-Age fort, dominates the exit of the lake. Dunmallet is formed of a tough rock known as the Basement Conglomerate, but elsewhere it is the more easily eroded mudstones, shales and slates of the Skiddaw Series that shape the landscape. This lower reach of Ullswater has been scoured out by ice working with great effect on these softer beds. In contrast, the other great rock formation of the Lake District, the Borrowdale Volcanic Series, gives rise to much more impressive landforms, including bare rock crags. Here it forms the towering backwall of Barton Fell which rises steeply from the eastern shores of the lake. The character of this volcanic country is best seen from the viewpoint on isolated Hallin Fell, which is approximately halfway along the southern shore. The beds of hardened tuffs,

The long dog-legged shape to Ullswater reflects the three distinct ice-eroded basins which together make up the lake. Much of the charm of the lake lies in the contrasting shores, sometimes gently shelving, other times steeply plunging into the deep dark waters especially around Hallin Fell

The constant appeal which the Lake District has for the ever-growing number of visitors stems largely from the rich variety of its scenery. Even its succession of lakes which radiate out from the central highlands like the spokes of a wheel, share in this variation.

Each is unique in its basin form, the setting of its shores, the character of its enclosing hills, and the relationship which it has to the surrounding area. The lakes, however, have one thing in common. They were all formed during the Ice Age as glaciers gouged out deep rock basins in the floors of pre-existing valleys. In some cases, notably Windermere, the glacier as it melted left behind a great dump of unsorted debris and this, too, has contributed to the formation of the lake.

The dog-legged form of Ullswater makes it different from other lakes. Except from the air, it is not possible to view the whole lake from end to end for there are marked changes of direction in its three reaches. To the north-east the

In its upper part Ullswater runs deep into the main central highland country of the Lake District overlooked by peaks like Sunday Crag and Place Fell

The second largest sheet of water in the Lake District with its shores much less developed than Windermere

ejected from ancient volcanoes, give rise to a succession of broken and weathered crags rising like steps from the lakeside in the vicinity of Howtown.

Further reading: Millward, R. and Robinson, A. H. W. *Cumbria* (Macmillan, 1973)

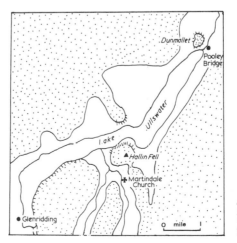

The twisting form of Ullswater between enclosing fingers of high land

39

Vestige of Arctic Britain: Cairngorms

The Cairngorms contain the largest area above 4,000ft (1,216m) in the British Isles. Although the area lacks permanent snow cover throughout the year, and would need to be about 1,000ft (300m) higher to experience it, the climate of the Cairngorms is our nearest approach to that found in much higher latitudes.

Not surprisingly, the latitude of the Cairngorms means a harsh climate throughout the year. For only five months a year, from May to October, does the mean temperature rise above freezing point. Even then the sunshine totals are very low and the persistent clouds give high humidity figures. The climatic parallel of the Cairngorm tops is with the coastal regions of the Arctic.

The Cairngorms was one of the last parts to be freed from the enveloping ice cover, when Northern Britain was just beginning to emerge from the Ice Age 10,000 years ago. As a result it became, and still is, a last refuge for both plants and animals which we would normally associate with the colder regions of the Arctic and high Alps. Little vegetation is able to survive in such a hostile environment and the wind velocities — twice as high as in neighbouring glens — mean that only prostrate plants can hope to grow. Much of the plateau top is covered with stony debris as the granite of the Cairngorms has been shattered by frost action of great intensity during the Ice Age and to a lesser extent right up to the present time. Only a few plants can colonise this stony waste. Chief among them is the woolly hair moss which

The western part of the Cairngorms is dominated by Braeriach and Cairn Toul, which rise to over 4,200 feet (1,280m). At such heights the tops are mostly covered in cloud and a distinctive vegetation has been able to survive in the adverse conditions. The view is of the corrie-lochan Uaine backed by the peak of Cairn Toul

forms a grey-green covering in those parts where the surface is sufficiently stable. In some places frost heaving during the winter months makes even this impossible and large stone patches are common. The recent development of the area for skiing has not helped, for the ski lifts bring thousands to the Cairngorm tops during the summer months. Continuous trampling along selected paths has destroyed the vegetation in many places so that conservation of this unique assemblage of plant types is a matter of high priority.

Fauna as well as flora show a marked response to the hostile 'Arctic' conditions of the highest parts around Braeriach (4,248ft, 1,291m). A species of Alpine sawfly, short-winged and flightless, is found only here. As it is incapable of extensive migration it seems that it must be a relic of former glacial conditions.

Further reading: Pearsall, W. H. *Mountains and Moorlands* (Collins, 1950)

Much of the top of the Cairngorms consists of a high-level plateau into which the ice has etched corrie basins and deep clefts like the valley of the Lairig Ghru

41

Coastal desert: Aberffraw dunes, Anglesey

In front of the main coastal dune belt a temporary fore-dune fringe develops as sand accumulates around piles of seaweed, and annual plants like the prickly saltwort colonise the tiny dunes

During winter many of the hollows between the linear dune ridges are occupied by shallow lakes. These dune slacks carry their own vegetation, mainly of creeping willow which flourishes in the damp conditions

Areas of sand dunes frequently occur around the coasts of Britain and are often given local names like towans, burrows or meols. They are most extensive when an adequate supply of sand is assured from a wide foreshore which lies in the path of the prevailing wind. The south-west coast of Anglesey meets these conditions and there are a number of dune areas, including that at Aberffraw.

The small, sleepy village of Aberffraw with its central square, perhaps betraying its former importance, was once the 'capital' of the Princes of Gwynedd. From their palace above the present village they must have looked out across the extensive sandy warren which was certainly there in early medieval times. The dunes were probably very active during the thirteenth and fourteenth centuries, for we know from the nearby Newborough Warren that the cutting of marram grass for making mats was stopped because it was leading to sand storms.

Because of the sterile nature of the sands and their capacity for swallowing rainfall, only certain plants can survive in these desert-like conditions. Marram grass, with its deep, ramifying system of roots, covers much of the dune surface. Near the sea it is a bright rich green for it is actively growing as fresh supplies of sand are added to the dunes. Further inland, where the dunes are more stable, the marram takes on a grey colour as it is unable to flourish in sands leached of their limited supply of nutrient minerals. The marram grass seldom forms a continuous sward on the more seaward of the dune belts and under certain conditions the wind has eroded great hollows or blowouts. The pattern of change constantly occurring means that the details of the dune landscape change from year to year. Even half a mile inland there is a belt of dunes being actively eroded on their seaward margin with sand carried over the dune crest and advancing inland over the area of flat links. Change and diversity are the characteristics of the Aberffraw dunes.

In between some of the dunes there are hollows filled with water, especially during the winter months when the lagoons can be up to 5ft (1½m) deep. By late spring the general level of the water table has fallen, the lagoons dry out and the floor is now covered by a mat of creeping willow. On the drier links the advancing summer brings the flowering of sweet-smelling thyme and the carpet of colour provided by heartsease.

Further reading: Hepburn, I. *Flowers of the Coast* (Collins, 1952)

The windward side of the central dune belt is under constant attack leading to a slow migration inland as the eroded sand is carried over the top

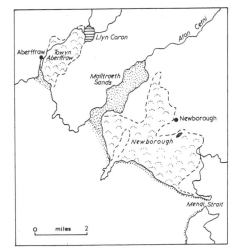

Extent of the main sand-dune areas in southern Anglesey

43

Coastline in retreat: Holderness, Yorkshire

Holderness is the fastest eroding coastline in the world. This is an expert's summing up of the present situation along this stretch of the Yorkshire coast from Bridlington in the north to Spurn in the south. There is every indication that the wearing back of the clay cliffs is taking place at a very rapid rate and has been doing so for many centuries. Accurate measurements, based on the position of the cliff face as shown on the Ordnance Survey map of 1852 and on subsequent editions right up to the present day, leave no doubt about the magnitude of the erosion. Although the rate is not always constant and varies from place to place, it can reach as much as 6ft (2m) a year on average.

Even erosion of half this amount, year after year, will lead to a considerable loss of land, including settlements built when the threat seemed far distant. We know that many villages listed in the Domesday Survey of 1086 have since been swept away. At the quiet seaside resort of Withernsea, now feeling secure behind its great concrete sea wall, the original parish church was destroyed by the sea in the early Middle Ages and had to be replaced in 1488 by a new building well inland. Farther south at Kilnsea, where the clay cliffs end and give way to the long causeway of sand running out to Spurn Point, the church was eaten away stone by stone between 1825 and 1831. Nowadays there is no

Dimlington Farm, where the clay cliffs are over 100ft (30m) high, has seen its land along the edge disappear at the rate of about 6ft (2m) a year over the past century

An attempt at Kilnsea to prevent erosion has met with little success and only the tangled remains of the former sea defences now stand

real village at Kilnsea, only an inn, chapel, and a few scattered houses arranged along the road which leads to Spurn. In some cases even the name of the village has gone as the whole parish has been consumed by the sea.

The continuous erosion of the Holderness coast is mainly due to the character of the cliffs themselves. They are almost entirely formed of clay which is subject to alternate wetting and drying out. This makes the cliff face unstable and leads to slides and slumps from above. The sea quickly removes the fallen debris on the beach and itself can attack the cliff base, steepening it and creating instability which in time leads to further collapse. Protection can be given but it is a costly operation which can only be justified at places like Withernsea and Hornsea where property rather than agricultural land is threatened. Even then protection is not assured and at Kilnsea the former concrete sea defences have been battered and reduced to rubble.

Further reading: Sheppard, T. *The Lost Towns of the Yorkshire Coast* (Brown, 1912)

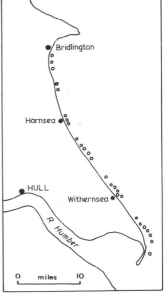

Villages which existed at the time of Domesday Book and have now fallen victims of the sea

Barmston, where the cliffs contain beds of sand as well as the ubiquitous clay, has made an unsuccessful attempt to resist the onslaught of the sea but all to no avail. Many of the bungalows shown in this 1973 photograph have now disappeared

45

Drowned valley: Christchurch Harbour, Hampshire

Spits enclose the present entrance to Christchurch Harbour, once a much wider and more open bay after the sea-level rise following the Ice Age had drowned the lower part of the Stour and Avon valleys

Like so many south-coast harbours Christchurch has become increasingly popular for sailing. Only a few fishermen now tend their nets at the harbour entrance at Mudeford and there is little commercial traffic in the port

Natural harbours have always proved of great value to man and the English Channel coastlands are particularly well-endowed. Deep-water ports like Southampton and Falmouth or lesser places like Poole and Christchurch owe their origin to the drowning of the lower courses of river valleys during the rise of sea level which began at the end of the Ice Age. The shape the harbour takes depends greatly on the form of the original valley before submergence. In the South-West Peninsula, the deeply set valleys give rise to long branching arms of the sea known as 'rias'.

In the case of Christchurch, the initial valley form was much more open and has led to the creation of a spacious, though relatively shallow harbour. The appearance of Christchurch varies

greatly depending on the state of the tide. When filled with water it forms a great expanse of blue which greatly enhances the setting of Christchurch Priory on its northern shores. When the tide is out the setting changes to one of bare mud-flats with only ribbons of water in the creeks. On its southern side Christchurch Harbour is dominated by the long hill of clay and ironstone running out to sea at Hengistbury Head. Its gorse and bracken-covered slopes are a popular walk either from Christchurch or Bournemouth. From its top there is a good view not only over the harbour but also along the coast westwards to the Isle of Purbeck or eastwards to the white cliffs of the Isle of Wight. The inner harbour is broad and spacious although its entrance at Mudeford Quay is enclosed by the growth of sandspits from opposing directions.

Prehistoric man found Hengistbury Head an easily defensible site and in the Bronze Age its dry, gravel-capped summit proved attractive to settlement. In the succeeding Iron Age a rampart and ditch system, known as the Double Dykes, was thrown across its narrow neck, the only really vulnerable approach. The sandspit running northwards from Hengistbury Head is the longest of the two that have grown up. In the past it grew to such an extent as to force the river channel to hug the cliffs for over a mile towards Highcliffe Castle. This development is unlikely to occur again for in recent years a great concrete promenade and car park have been built over the former river exit-channel at Mudeford Beach. Only at Mudeford Quay, with its old fishermen's cottages and inn, is there any link with the past.

Further reading: Fowler, P. *Wessex, (Regional Archaeologies)* (Heinemann Educational, 1967)

Hengistbury Head is mainly composed of sand and clay beds but there are lines of ironstone doggers running through and these give the teeth which enable the headland to resist erosion

47

Fenland relic: Wicken Fen, Cambridgeshire

Part of Adventurer's Fen
with its sedge, rushes and
flowering iris flourishing in
the damp habitat. The re-
assembled Fenland mill was
originally the only means of
lifting water from the field
drains into the higher level of
the main channel

One of the many artificial
channels or lodes which are
used to drain Wicken Fen

Both nature and man have contrived to make the Fenland one of the most distinctive regions of Britain. It is the largest lowland area in the country covering over 2,000 sq miles (5,180sq km). For the most part, except for a few raised islands of gravel, it is below the level of high spring tides and therefore has to be protected by sea walls. An even greater problem arises from the fact that the inner part of the Fenland, composed of dark peat, lies at a lower level than the more seaward section formed of silt.

Drainage has always presented major difficulties and when the natural rivers like the Ouse, Nene and Welland proved unequal to the task, man had to intervene. A great phase of drainage activity began in the seventeenth century largely under the guidance of Dutch experts like Vermuyden. Straight cuts like the Bedford Level were made to carry the fen waters more directly to the sea and windmills were introduced to lift the water from the lower levels into the major drains. The transformation achieved by the Dutch engineers and their successors was remarkable and what was once the domain of fish, fowl and fur became the richest farmland of the whole country. Cereals, potatoes and especially market garden produce grow well on both the peat and silt soils.

So highly prized was the drained land that most of the original fen of reeds and sedges quickly disappeared so that today only one or two small pockets remain to give us an impression of its original character. One such area is Wicken Sedge Fen lying approximately halfway between Ely and Newmarket. This was never drained and cleared for it formed the common of the village of Wicken. The Fen is now under the guardianship of the National Trust who look upon it as an open-air laboratory where changes in the fauna and flora of this unique 'wet' land can be studied. Running through the centre is the major drainage channel of Wicken Lode and this effectively divides the area into the untamed sedge fen to the north and the

Adventurer's Fen to the south. There is thus an immediate contrast between the 'natural' and the man-made landscape. Each area takes us back into the past for even in the tamed Adventurer's Fen a windmill has been erected to provide a link with the time when it was the sole means of power to lift the water from the lower drains, an operation upon which the whole success of the drainage scheme depended.

A mid-seventeenth-century map prepared at the time when the Dutchman Vermuyden was carrying out his great scheme of reclaiming the Fens based on the construction of a major drainage channel, the Bedford Level. It was Vermuyden's work that completely transformed the appearance of the original Fenland, hence the importance of relict areas like Wicken

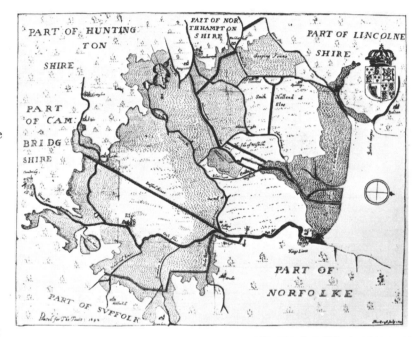

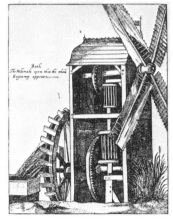

A diagram of an early wind-driven water pump on which the early sixteenth-century drainage schemes depended

Further reading: Astbury, A. K. *The Black Fens* (County History Reprints, Educational Productions, 1958)

Sea stacks and geos: Duncansby, Caithness

The cliff coastline immediately to the south of Duncansby Head at the north-east corner of the Scottish mainland, is justly regarded as one of the finest stretches in the whole of the British Isles. The reason for its grandeur is not difficult to understand for its cliffs of flagstone and sandstone have been carved into a multiplicity of shapes as they have responded to the relentless attacks of the sea over thousands of years.

Geos

Immediately to the south of Duncansby the line of the cliff wall is broken by a narrow, deeply cut inlet. This is one of many similar features which are found along the whole length of the Caithness coast. They are known locally as 'geos' and nearly always develop where the rock, whether it be sandstone, flagstone or conglomerate, has been fractured by earth movements and in consequence forms a narrow belt of shattered, weakened beds. It is these which the sea is able to exploit most readily and in time it will entirely remove the whole zone of fractured

The famous spire stacks of Duncansby Bay where weathering has created pinnacles of rock with the sea constantly attacking the base. In some cases the sea has reduced the former stack to a mere rock at sea level

A flat-topped stack at Duncansby fashioned from horizontally bedded flag-stones

Where the sea is able to exploit a band of shattered rock due to faulting, a narrow inlet or geo develops

rock. The walls of the geo are consequently abrupt and steep. From above, the inlet looks dark and forbidding with the ceaseless rumble of the sea indicating that it is still carrying on with its work of selective erosion. The geo is but one element which contributes to the total harmony of this impressive section of the Caithness coast.

Sea stacks

A few hundred yards to the south of the geo the setting alters as the rock type changes from flagstone to sandstone. The cliffs are multi-coloured with the red sandstone being streaked with greys and browns as well as covered with patches of green where the salt-loving plants have gained a footing. In front of the general line of cliffs there are isolated pinnacles of rock (stacks) of various shapes and sizes. Many have pointed tops so that they resemble spires, a distinctive form which makes the Duncansby 'cathedral' stacks both impressive and unique. The presence of stacks implies that coast erosion has been taking place over a long period of time. At first the sea would penetrate the cliff line along parallel geos. As these were enlarged the rocky peninsula between two adjacent inlets would become narrow. If cave systems were then able to link up two geos, ultimately a natural arch would develop. The collapse of this would leave only an isolated column of rock, the stack standing out in front of the new line of the coast.

Further reading: Steers, J. A. *The Coastline of Scotland* (Cambridge University Press, 1973)

The natural arch, again in flagstones, formed as the sea has enlarged a cave cut into a small headland. In time the bridge will collapse to give a stack

Surrey heathland: the Devil's Jumps, Surrey

The fluted ironstone capping which creates the conical hills known as the Devil's Jumps near Churt

Frensham Great Pond has the appearance of a natural body of water set amidst the heathland but in reality it is artificial, the creation of the nearby Waverley Abbey where it served as a source of fish

The scenery of the Surrey heaths is surprisingly rich and varied in places. Near Churt, 5 miles (8km) south of Farnham, three conical hills known as the Devil's Jumps have long attracted attention. In the last century they presented something of a puzzle, but we now know that they owe their origin to a capping of resistant ironstone. William Cobbett, the traveller and political commentator who was born at Farnham could only write: 'For my part I cannot account for this placing of these hills. How could waters rolling about form such hills? How could such hills have bubbled up from beneath? But in short, it is all wonderful alike.' The present generation cannot but agree with this sentiment.

Attitudes and ideas can often change dramatically with time. In the last century the Surrey heaths were looked upon as wastelands which were quite unresponsive to the efforts of the agricultural improver. They were also

looked upon as natural features which had developed because of the sandy rocks with which they are closely associated. Here was an untamed landscape of heather, gorse, bracken, the occasional silver birch and stunted oak. What was the despair of past generations has now become the salvation of the present for the open vistas now provide a much-prized 'lung' for the town dweller. The countryside of commons between Farnham and Hindhead is especially valued in this respect. The presence of a broad band of pure sands, the Folkestone Beds, is largely responsible, for it gives rise to sterile and heavily leached, silver-grey soils completely lacking in humus. The heathy wilderness is ideal for recreation and around Frensham the Great and Little Ponds — artificial lakes created to serve as fish hatcheries for nearby Waverley Abbey — offer facilities for boating and sailing.

It would be easy to dismiss the heaths as the natural response to unfavourable geological conditions. This would be an over-simplification, however, for recently it has been suggested that prehistoric man is partly responsible for their present character. By clearing away its light forest cover, perhaps over 4,000 years ago, he prevented the soils from obtaining a natural supply of humus from leaf fall. The naturally sandy soils soon became even more leached and sterile, fit only to support a vegetation of heather, gorse and bracken.

Further reading: Millward, R. and Robinson, A. H. W. *South East England – Thameside and Weald* (Macmillan, 1971)

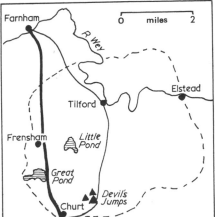

The heavily leached sandy soil, know as podsol, predominates over much of the area with bands of flat ironstone developed through the concentration of iron salts at certain horizons. Lacking in humus and poor in mineral salts the soil carries only a poor heath and scrub vegetation, though it will respond to good farming management

Sandy heath country lying south of Farnham

53

Neolithic settlement: Skara Brae, Orkney

More than a century ago, an Atlantic storm uncovered the remains of stone-built huts among the sand dunes of Skail Bay on the western shore of Orkney's largest island, Mainland. Excavations of the site between 1927 and 1930 and again in 1972 unravelled the details of its history. Skara Brae has since been described as preserving 'the most striking remains of Neolithic settlement in Britain' and as 'unique in northern Europe', because the original furnishings of its sunken huts among the dunes are preserved in stone.

The settlement, a Stone-Age village, belongs to the late Neolithic. It was inhabited in the centuries between 1000BC and 1500BC. Among the abundant finds from Skara Brae are polished stone axes, rough stone knives, utensils of whalebone, and coarse elaborately grooved pottery that belongs to a type known widely from the middle and late Neolithic sites in Britain. Some of the designs in the pottery as well as the spiral motifs in carving among the stones of the settlement suggest links

The complex of stone-built dwellings that lay buried until the middle of the nineteenth century among the sand dunes on the edge of Skail Bay in the west of Orkney's largest island

is the reproduction of the equipment of everyday life in the same stone. On each side of the tunnel-like entrance are beds constructed from stone slabs. Recesses in the walls acted as cupboards and each house contained a stone dresser. On one of the stone dressers the excavators discovered a pot still standing — a mysterious relic of life in the cold north of Britain more than 3,000 years ago.

Further reading: Bailey, Patrick *Orkney* (David & Charles, 1972)

Inside one of the huts at Skara Brae. The walls are built of carefully fitted thin stone slabs. In the centre is a raised hearth and, perhaps the most striking object of all, a piece of Neolithic furniture in stone is the 'dresser' that stands against the wall

(below) The architecture of the late Neolithic in Orkney at Maeshowe. The central chamber of this prehistoric tomb reveals the high technical skills of early man in northern Britain as he worked in stone

with Neolithic sites in Ireland and Iberia. Prehistoric settlers probably reached the lonely shores of the Bay of Skail as part of a long movement that colonised many parts of western Britain from the Irish Sea to the Hebrides.

Three main stages of occupation and building have been recognised at Skara Brae. In its final phase the village consisted of six stone huts sunk in the sand dunes and connected by covered passageways. The whole, a prehistoric human warren, was covered with a midden of ash, dung and broken bones. Living beneath an accumulation of their own refuse the Neolithic pastoralists of Skara Brae found shelter from the searing winds of these northern isles. Each of the half dozen houses consisted of a single room, square in shape, and some 15ft (5m) across. The walls are carefully built of close-fitting, thin stone slabs and at the centre is a raised hearth where a peat fire burned. The most remarkable feature of Skara Brae

Hebridean prehistory: Callanish, Isle of Lewis

The standing stones of Callanish, gaunt and grey, crown the summit of a slightly raised mound in western Lewis. This monument, only rivalled by Stonehenge in all Britain, was buried beneath a thick layer of growing peat until it was excavated towards the end of the nineteenth century

Close to the head of East Loch Roag, a remote fjord of the Outer Hebrides, are the remains of an elaborate stone circle that may well be described as the Stonehenge of northern Britain. Near the centre of the circle that is almost 40ft (12m) across stands a tall thin megalith, a shimmering grey blade of stone that reaches almost 16ft (5m) in height. The circle itself is made up of thirteen similar slabs of stone, averaging a height of 10ft (3m). But this 'henge' monument of the remote Outer Hebrides has other puzzling and complex features. To the north runs an avenue of standing stones that once might have had twenty monoliths radiated to east and west of the circle. Lastly, to the east of the focal central pillar there is a chambered cairn, a prehistoric burial place composed of slabs of stone.

Even the date of the raising of the stones of Callanish remains obscure; the discovery of its true purpose has scarcely passed beyond the realms of speculation. The Scottish stone circles and other megalithic objects of the northern landscape lie within the time span of 2700-1300BC. The date of the

building of Callanish is probably within the last 500 years of that long period.

All speculations about the Stone-Age circles are tentative, based on the partial remains of a long-lost prehistoric culture. The great stone circles of western Europe have long been thought of as places of worship and ritual temples. Callanish with its burial cairn has been described as 'an original fusion of tomb and temple'. But lately views have been expressed that the circle and its avenue of standing stones have been placed in relation to the risings and settings of the sun and moon at particular seasons. It has been noticed that the avenue of stones, looking southwards, points to the distant skyline of the mountains of Harris. The avenue is aligned on Clisham, the highest peak, behind which the setting of the midsummer moon occurs. Other intricate connections between the stones and the heavens have been proposed in this thesis, and it has been suggested that the thirteen stones composing the main circle could have been designed to form the basis of a lunar calendar. Callanish, as Gerald Hawkins has written, 'seems to have been used primarily to establish a calendar, though it may possibly have been used for predicting eclipses as well'. There are twelve large stones and one small; they could have been used to mark the short years of twelve lunar months and the long of thirteen months.

Further reading: Hawkins, G. S. *Stonehenge Decoded,* Appendix C (Fontana Books, 1970) *Callanish, A Scottish Stonehenge* (Souvenir Press, 1966)

The central megalith of Callanish, a blade of grey rock standing almost 16ft (5m) in height

Megalithic monument: Stonehenge, Wiltshire

A 'temple' and place of sacrifice in the minds of Victorian antiquarians; more recent research has revealed a deep knowledge of mathematics and astronomy in its construction. The insignificant stones of the 'bluestone' circle may be discerned among the huge megaliths of the sarsen stones.

Stonehenge stands on the chalk plateau of Salisbury Plain, at the very heart of prehistoric England. Without doubt it is the greatest building of British prehistory, one to which the term architecture can properly be applied. Stonehenge lies amidst a countryside of gentle chalk hills rich with remains of the New Stone Age and the Bronze Age. In the vicinity are some 300 Bronze-Age burial mounds and not far away are the magnificent earthworks of Avebury and Silbury Hill.

Myths and legends have surrounded Stonehenge for many long centuries. Not surprisingly, for it is a complex monument, planned and shaped over a span of 500 years, between 1900BC and 1400BC, and today its existence gives rise to numerous new theories concerning the mysteries that its precision of

structure invites. Among the earliest references is that from Geoffrey of Monmouth in his *Historia Regum Britanniae* (*c* 1136) with the legend that the stones were magically transported from Ireland by Merlin! The connection of Stonehenge with the Druids has held public imagination since the seventeenth century, but this popular theory is as yet without foundation. Deep obscurity surrounds the prehistoric purpose of Stonehenge and the presence of the Altar Stone, Slaughter Stone and excavated cremated human bones lends itself to the theory that it was a place where Bronze-Age ceremonies and religious rites took place. Modern interpretation of the monument is chiefly based on the excavations by the Society of Antiquaries of London, since 1919. Recent research has described it as a prehistoric 'astronomical observatory' that could be used as a 'digital computing machine'.

Structure

Stonehenge consists of a number of structural elements, mostly circular in plan, as shown in the diagram. It appears to have evolved in three main stages, beginning with a perimeter bank and ditch dating from the late Neolithic period, soon after 2000BC. The monument was completed in the century following 1500BC. Two totally different types of rock have been hewn to shape Stonehenge's monoliths. The pale silvery-grey stones that make up its dominating elements — the huge upright stones of the outer circle supporting the carefully shaped and gently curved horizontal slabs — come from the locality. These are all 'sarsens', whose nearest probable source is the surface of the downs near Avebury. The large features of the horseshoe at the core of the monument are of the same material. Within the outer ring of Stonehenge stands an insignificant circle of 'bluestones', of a distinctive rock which geological analysis has shown can only be from the Prescelly Hills in distant Pembrokeshire. It is clear that the bluestones were erected after the sarsens, since some of them stand in the filling of the ramps of the sarsens' sockets. Much speculation has been directed at how the bluestones arrived at Stonehenge for the distance from Pembrokeshire is 240 miles (387km). Each stone weighs 5 tons (5 tonnes) and originally there were fifty of them in the outer circle. Recent work suggests that another structure of bluestones stood about a mile (1½km) north-west of Stonehenge and that they were brought to Wiltshire in the late Neolithic period, some centuries before their erection in their present position.

Further reading: Atkinson, R. J. C. *Stonehenge* (Pelican Books, 1960) Hawkins, G. S. *Stonehenge Decoded* (Fontana Books, 1970)

Sarsen stones in situ
Bluestones in situ
Former stones

The stone rings of Stonehenge

The pages of Camden's *Britannia* provide a seventeenth-century view of Stonehenge

An outcrop of dolerite on the summit of the Prescelly Hills, the same rock out of which the 'bluestones' of Stonehenge were shaped. Mystery still envelops the problem of the mode of transport of this rock from western Wales to Salisbury Plain. To add to the ingenious speculations of archaeologists, a geologist has now suggested that the stones reached the chalk country transported as erratics by an eastward-moving ice-sheet

Roman frontier: the Roman Wall, Northumberland

The north-facing scarp of the Whin Sill near Broomlee Lough provides a ready-made natural setting for the wall which hugs its crest for many miles

For much of its length the original wall has been removed as later generations found the shaped stones ideal for building farmhouses and barns. In this section east of Housesteads the main road runs along the line of the original wall. It is fronted by a ditch while, behind, a similar feature known as the vallum can be clearly traced on the ground.

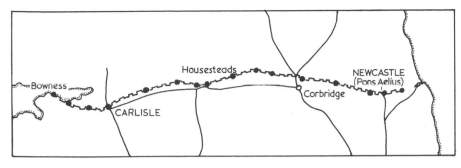

It is not always appreciated that the Roman Wall, stretching for 73 miles (117km) from the Solway to the Tyne, represents one of the finest monuments to the greatness of the Roman Empire not only in Britain but in northern Europe as a whole. Begun in AD122, following a visit by the Emperor Hadrian, it took over eight years to complete. With its associated great ditch on its north side and another with ramparts — the vallum — within it to the south, the wall forms an impressive barrier and show of strength. At regularly spaced intervals there were mile-castles and, at strategic places major points which housed the garrisons.

The centuries have taken their toll of the remains of the wall for it provided an easily accessible quarry for later buildings. In the central section around Housesteads, about 8 miles (13km) west of Hexham, there is a wealth of remains which show nearly every aspect of the defensive system as well as providing an insight into the life of the soldiers stationed in this hostile border country. The wall itself is well preserved as it follows the contours of the top of the escarpment formed by the hard igneous rock of the Whin Sill. In some places this is so steep as to make the wall itself seem unnecessary. It was nevertheless built and maintained as a continuous unit. Behind, but close to the wall, lay the major fort of Housesteads, occupying many acres of the gently sloping ground to the south. Here the rectangular outline is well-preserved as well as the remains within it: a headquarters building, barracks, a granary, baths and latrines. Some civilian buildings apparently lay outside the fort with plots where crops could be grown. It seems unlikely that the fort was ever self-supporting. The site can be visited quite easily from the B6318 road and in addition to the remains on the ground there is a small museum.

Four miles (6km) to the east, at Carrawburgh, there is another fort, Broccolita, with its grassy ramparts betraying its outline but largely unexcavated as yet. Close by in a shallow valley, a temple to the pagan god Mithras has recently been uncovered and this gives another indication of the life led by the soldiers who were brought here to defend the wall against raids from the north.

Further reading: Philipson, J., (ed) *Northumberland National Park* – Countryside Commission (H.M.S.O., 1969)

A reconstructed section of the wall though not raised to its original height. Hundreds of masons were employed in the building of the wall over a seven-year period, shaping the local stone to fit together with the minimum of mortar

Celtic Christianity: Iona, Argyll

The restored medieval abbey buildings at Iona, on a site where Columba founded a monastery in the sixth century. Across the mile-wide channel of translucent green sea the abbey faces the island of Mull with its rough granite hills and, in the background, the high basalt sea cliffs of the volcanic country

A Dark-Age cross, elaborately carved in granite, stands before the abbey church

Iona, a tiny island of grey gneiss rocks, lies off the westernmost peninsula of Mull separated by a sea strait only a mile (1½km) wide.

History

The island became the earliest settlement of the Christian church in northern and western Scotland when Columba sailed there from Ireland in AD563 to found a monastery.

Adamnan, an abbot of Iona about AD700, records in his *Life of St Columba* how the monastery on the island became the centre from which the mainland Picts were converted to the Christian church. In the early seventh century, Iona played an equally important part in the history of Christianity in northern England through its daughter house at Lindisfarne.

The Viking raids in the ninth and tenth centuries brought the monastic communities of Scotland close to extinction. The Dark-Age monastery at Iona — a cluster of huts and simple wooden buildings — was burnt to the ground on several occasions. The

62

records tell of its destruction in 795. In 802 the monastery was rebuilt but razed to the ground in 806, and again in 825. But despite the ravages of the Vikings, the records suggest that a Celtic community continued in Iona until the beginning of the thirteenth century when Reginald, son of Somerled, Lord of the Isles, founded a Benedictine abbey there.

Iona remained outside the diocesan structure of the rest of the British Isles until the fifteenth century. It had been joined to the Scandinavian world under the Archbishops of Trondheim. By the end of the fifteenth century the medieval abbey had fallen into ruins, but in the year 1500, when the abbey was chosen to become the cathedral of the bishopric of the Isles, rebuilding began once more.

The late sixteenth century and the Reformation brought another dark age to Iona. In 1574 the abbey and its properties were seized by MacLean of Duart and a century later it passed to Campbell of Argyll. The buildings of the medieval abbey were abandoned; roofless they faced the Atlantic winter gales. Even so the holy qualities of Iona were not completely lost. When Dr Johnson visited the island in the eighteenth century on his famous tour of the Hebrides, he wrote: 'that man is little to be envied whose piety would not grow warmer among the ruins of Iona'.

Another renaissance began in this rocky, treeless, grey-white island when the 8th Duke of Argyll gave the roofless buildings of the abbey to the Iona Trustees of the Church of Scotland in the year 1899. By 1965 more than half a century of restoration had been completed and now, under the inspiration of Lord Macleod of Fiunary, Iona has once more become a place of spiritual renewal amid the materialism of the twentieth century.

Further reading: Murray, W. H. *Islands of Western Scotland: Inner and Outer Hebrides* (Eyre Methuen, 1973)

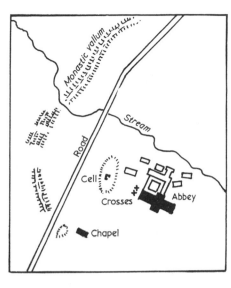

Layout of the monastic site at Iona

The cult of St Columba with the ancient churches and parishes bearing his name

The oldest surviving ruins on Iona are the remains of the nunnery built by Reginald, son of Somerled, Lord of the Isles, in the thirteenth century. Of pink stone they have a lustrous beauty

Kingdom of Northumbria: Bamburgh, Northumberland

An isolated outcrop of the Whin Sill on the coast forms an ideal setting for the defensive works around which the original 'capital' of the kingdom developed

Each and every view of Bamburgh is spectacular. Seen from the seaward, with the white sand dunes piled against the bare volcanic crag of the castle, it suggests an impregnable fortress. The same is true of the view from the village green. Here the long black ridge of rock effectively seals off the approach from the south giving security for the settlement which grew up at its foot. The Angles who landed here in the sixth century were immediately attracted to the site for it gave them a strong-point on the coast from which to gain territory farther inland.

Within forty years the Angles had established themselves between the Tyne and the Forth and created the kingdom of Northumbria with Bamburgh as its capital. For over 300 years the kingdom had a powerful voice in the affairs of the country as a whole and successive kings like Ethelfrith, Edwin and Oswald wielded considerable influence, not least in the spread of Christianity. Since its

initial royal status, time has dealt harshly with the fortunes of Bamburgh. The original Anglian settlement was probably on the castle rock itself, but even this was not safe from the plundering raids of the Danes who ultimately brought about the downfall of the kingdom. After the Norman Conquest there was a period of relative calm and a town of cottages grew up between the castle and church. In medieval times the town had market rights, the present green being the site of the market place. To arrest its decline Bamburgh even tried to develop a port, Bamburgh Newtown, on the shores of Budle Bay a mile (1½km) away to the north-west. For a time it appeared that the experiment would be successful for Henry II even granted the burgesses of the port the same rights as the citizens of Newcastle. Competition from Berwick ultimately led to its collapse and today only a single farmhouse marks the site of the failed port.

Present-day Bamburgh

Today peace and tranquility are all that Bamburgh has to offer. The burgh has shrunk to a small green village, largely laid out by Lord Crewe at the beginning of the nineteenth century. Even the castle has undergone restoration and conversion into apartments, mainly by Lord Armstrong in 1890. For all this, Bamburgh still has the air of a 'royal city', the designation given to it by the Venerable Bede.

Further reading: White, J. T. *The Scottish Border and Northumberland* (Eyre Methuen, 1973)

The present castle, extensively rebuilt in the nineteenth century by the industrialist Lord Armstrong, completely dominates the linear village of Bamburgh with its former small triangular market place and church at the far end

Dark-Age frontier: Offa's Dyke, Shropshire

History is clearly written on the present landscape where Offa's Dyke, thrown up in the latter half of the eighth century, crosses a lowland among the hills of the Welsh Marches near Montgomery. The long established use of the dyke as a property boundary shows up in the sharp edge of the wood in the middle distance and its function as a base line in the modern field pattern

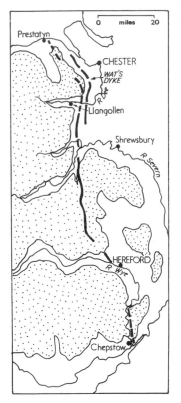

Offa's Dyke, the political frontier of the Midland kingdom of Mercia

Down the succeeding centuries Offa's Dyke has played a role in the evolution of the landscape of the Welsh Marches. It has been used as a landmark for county and parish boundaries and it delimits the territories of scores of estates and farms. In places it boldly marches across hillsides with wide commanding views into Wales but elsewhere, particularly in the lowland by Montgomery, the line of the earthwork completely ignores the strategic advantages of overshadowing hills to the west. The location of Offa's Dyke must have been determined also by the political geography of the time; it seems to have been a negotiated line between Mercia and the Welsh powers to the west — Gwynedd, Powys and Gwent.

The Saxon kingdom of the Midlands, Mercia, reached the heights of political power in the eighth century under its rulers Aethelbald (AD716-57) and his successor, Offa, who died in 796. From the secular and ecclesiastical capitals at Tamworth and Lichfield in the central Midlands the power of eighth-century Mercia reached into southern England, northwards to an uncertain frontier with Northumbria and westwards into the hills of the Welsh border country. Through the marchland with Wales two great earthworks were thrown up to define the western frontier of Mercia. Wat's Dyke, probably built early in Aethelbald's reign, crosses the lowland and foothills of the most vulnerable part of Mercia's borderland between Holywell and Oswestry. Offa's Dyke was constructed towards the end of the eighth century, most likely in the closing years of the king's reign between 784 and 796. It is mentioned in Bishop Asser's *Life of King Alfred*, written scarcely more than a century later. Asser describes the earthwork, a bank averaging 6ft (2m) in height, with a flanking ditch, as running 'the whole way from sea to sea'. This was from the mouth of the Dee, near Prestatyn, to the place where the Wye empties into the Severn close to Chepstow. The length of the dyke is 149 miles (238km). Eight summers of detailed field research between 1925 and 1932 on every mile of the earthwork by the archaeologist Sir Cyril Fox showed some important incomplete sections. At the northern end 16 miles (25km) were never built and there is a long break in the plain of Herefordshire where, for 37 miles (59km), the river Wye seems to have served as a frontier. No documen-

tary evidence survives to tell of the engineering problems and the organisation of labour in the making of the earthwork but Fox, from a careful and imaginative study of the field evidence, has concluded that Offa's Dyke is much more than a defensive earthwork with purely military functions.

Further reading: Fox, Sir Cyril *Offa's Dyke* (Oxford University Press, 1955)

Offa's Dyke in the hill-country to the north of Bishop's Castle. A sunken lane now occupies the ditch on the western flank of the earthwork, a hollow that was originally excavated as a source of earth and stone for the original building of the dyke

67

Dark-Age Christianity: Deerhurst, Gloucestershire

In a secluded corner of Gloucestershire on the bank of the Severn stands a church with a long and complex history in the centuries before the Norman Conquest. Its most striking external feature is the tall, narrow late Saxon tower. The lines of herringbone masonry in the nave and tower are another early architectural theme

Odda's Chapel lies only a few hundred yards from St Mary's Deerhurst and the site of the Saxon monastery. Its origins and true purpose remained unknown until work in the kitchen of this timber-framed farmhouse revealed the chapel that dated from just before the Norman Conquest

Deerhurst occupies a secluded site on the east bank of the Severn some 4 miles (6km) below Tewkesbury.

Before the Norman Conquest it possessed an important Saxon monastery of the Benedictine Order. The date of the monastic foundation is unknown but it has been argued, mainly from some architectural features surviving in the parish church of St Mary at Deerhurst and obscure references in the *Life of St Samson of Dol*, written before AD600, that Christianity at Deerhurst reaches back before the Saxon settlement of the West Country to the age of the Celtic saints. St Samson, Bishop of South Wales in the first half of the sixth century and founder of many churches in Cornwall and Brittany, is credited with the establishment of the first

monastic community at Deerhurst.

Two buildings, the parish church and Odda's Chapel, take the mind back into the Saxon centuries at Deerhurst. Recently the excavation of the ruined chancel behind the present church has shown a complex building history before the Norman Conquest. Six major stages are recognised. Fragments of Roman pottery and tiles suggest that the first Saxon church was raised over the site of a Roman villa. The plain rectangular shape of the present church, narrow and seemingly immensely tall, probably contains much of the structure of a Saxon stone church that must have been in existence by the beginning of the ninth century, when the monastery at Deerhurst briefly enters the light of history. It may well be much older. Some of its most ancient features are the strange, high triangular-shaped openings in the north, south and west walls of the nave. They may represent the windows of the original primitive

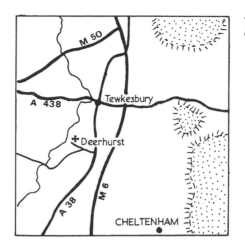

The location of the Saxon church of Deerhurst

church. Also there is a pair of triangular headed windows that look down on to the nave from the interior of the tower, doorways composed of megalithic blocks, and the ancient technique of herring-bone masonry surviving in the walls. In the later Saxon period, the tenth century, the church was extended with a chancel that ended in a circular apse, and a huge chancel arch that has since been blocked up was inserted in the eastern wall of the older church.

St Mary's with its strangely primitive Saxon tower stands only a few hundred yards from a little late Saxon church, Odda's Chapel. This building forms part of a half-timbered farmhouse where it remained undiscovered until 1885. Then, with the house under repair, the removal of plaster revealed an ancient window. Further investigation showed that the room that was used as a kitchen was in fact the nave of a Saxon chapel. In 1965 the chapel was disentangled from the farmhouse and now stands as one of the most complete small Saxon churches in the country, its dedication dated to 1056.

The base of the tall, narrow Saxon church tower at Deerhurst with its courses of Herringbone masonry and evidence of re-used decorated stones from some earlier building

Further reading: Finberg, H. P. R. *Gloucestershire – The Making of the English Landscape* (Hodder, 1975)

Lost borough: Dunwich, Suffolk

Soft sands readily attacked by the sea and the crumbling cliffline have taken their toll of the once important town of Dunwich. Most of the original town has disappeared including its many churches. All Saints, the last to go, has some flint masonry remains on the beach

(inset) An isolated gravestone in the former churchyard of All Saints, now lying forlorn amidst the scrub of the cliff top

Dunwich is a town with a long history but with few remains to show for it. As early as AD630 Bishop Felix founded his episcopal see on this lonely stretch of the Suffolk coast. The religious settlement quickly grew into a sizeable town and by the time of the Domesday Survey of 1086 it had a recorded population of over a thousand. The prosperity of the place is shown by the fact that it had three churches and paid an annual tax of 68,000 herrings. During the reign of Henry II it was still spoken of as 'a town of good note, already with much riches and sundry kinds of merchandizes'. But already the erosion of the coastline was beginning to take its toll. With the steady nibbling away of the soft cliffs of sand and loam more and more of the town fell into the sea. St

Michael's Church disappeared in 1331, followed by St Leonard's sometime after 1350, St Martin's and St Nicholas later in the same century. By 1540 the sea had reached the edge of the market place. We have an accurate picture of the disappearance of the town from Elizabeth's reign onwards, for in 1587 a local surveyor, Ralph Agas, produced a detailed map of Dunwich showing its remaining streets and buildings. The map was reproduced by Thomas Gardner in his history of the town in 1753 and the coastline of this date was added. This showed that between 1587 and 1753 the coastline had retreated by as much as 5ft (2m) a year on average. Since Gardner's day, the rate of erosion has lessened to about half this figure but even so the continual loss has

Former streets of the town are no more than narrow leafy sunken lanes leading to the cliff edge

(below) Thomas Gardner's view of the town as he sketched it for his book the *History of Dunwich* published in 1753

(bottom) Gardner also included a map based on a street plan prepared by Ralph Agas in 1589 in which he added the coastline as it existed in 1753. This showed how much of the town had disappeared between 1589 and his time. Much of the remaining part of the town has succumbed since so that today perhaps only a quarter of the original site exists

effectively removed another great slice of the former town. Not surprisingly Dunwich lost its borough charter in 1832 after holding it for over 600 years.

Today Dunwich is but a shadow of its former self. Shaded and overgrown sunken lanes ending abruptly at the cliff top mark the lines of the original streets where these have not already been destroyed. The occasional gravestone from the cemetery of All Saints – the last of the churches to go in 1913 – sometimes comes to light amidst the thicket and scrub covering part of the now deserted cliff top. Down below on the beach are masses of flint rubble from the walls of the former church. The sea, taking its toll, leaves little by way of tangible remains and it would be useless for the underwater archaeologist to search for anything offshore.

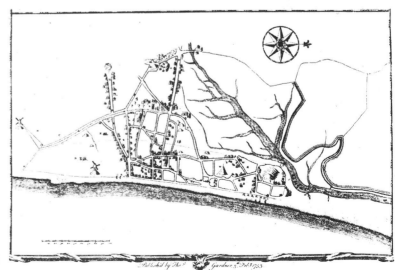

Further reading: Seymour, J. *Companion Guide to East Anglia* (Collins, 1970)

Edwardian castle towns: Criccieth and Harlech, Gwynedd

The original medieval features of the town of Criccieth

The isolated hard rock promontory which forms a natural setting for a coastal fortress at Criccieth was favoured first by the Welsh prince Llewelyn and then taken over by Edward I. The original small town was laid out on the landward site with burgage plots arranged around a tiny market place

The mountain mass of Snowdonia for long proved an ideal retreat of the Welsh princes, and sporadic attempts by Norman and Plantagenet kings to subdue the area met with little success. It was left to Edward I in the closing years of the thirteenth century to devise an effective means of control. A ring of castle towns or bastides was established around the mountainous heart and English settlers were encouraged to become burgesses. It is a measure of the astuteness of Edward in choosing his sites that Denbigh, Flint, Conway, Harlech, Caernarvon, Criccieth and Beaumaris still exist as urban centres.

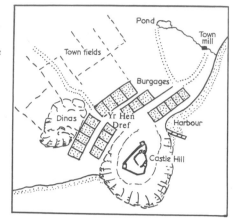

Criccieth

At Criccieth, Edward could take advantage of an already existing Welsh castle perched high on a promontory formed of tough, orange-coloured felsite rock. Masons and materials were brought in through the small harbour close by and a programme of rebuilding took place in 1282. In the next two years a small town grew up on the landward side of the castle on the relatively flat ground between it and another rocky crag, Dinas. Burgage plots were laid out, each measuring a standard 80ft x 60ft (24m x 18m), for the settlers from England. Beyond lay the town fields where they could grow their subsistence crops. Although the passing centuries have modified the original medieval plan it is still possible to seek out features which take us back 700 years to the formative period of this small bastide town. In Yr Hen Dref — the old town — the tiny market place nestles by the castle gate with its cottages still occupying the original burgage plots. Surviving field names like Y Llathen and Y Ddwy Lathen date back to the initial allocation of land in the town field because *llathern* is a unit of holding broadly corresponding to the English virgate. Down by the harbour there is a cottage known as Hen Felin, which is built on the site of the town's original corn mill.

Harlech

Across the ruffled waters of Tremadog Bay, Criccieth Castle looks out to Harlech, another Edwardian fortress town. The castle, set high on a rocky bluff overlooking the marshes and sand dunes of Morfa Harlech, is even more impressive and completely dominates the small town, whose narrow straggling streets have had to wrestle with an unfavourable site. Harlech, too, once had its small harbour at the foot of the castle crag, but the passing centuries have completely transformed a geographical setting that once served Edward's purpose so well.

Further reading: Lewis, E. A. *The Medieval Boroughs of Snowdonia* (University of Wales Press, 1912)

(above) **Harlech, dominated by its Edwardian castle, is set on top of what was once the coastal cliff. Now it overlooks an area of marshland and sand dunes with the sea more than a mile away. As at Criccieth a small town of narrow streets is huddled around the massive castle walls**

The ring of castle towns, or bastides, established by Edward I

Fact or fiction: the Roman Steps and Rhinogs, Gwynedd

The carefully laid slabs forming the so-called Roman Steps mark out a trackway which climbs steadily towards the col through the Rhinog Range

The rocky terrain inland from Harlech, culminating in the twin summits of the Rhinogs, is as bare of people as its highest parts are bare of vegetation. This was not always the case.

Amidst its deep heather and half-buried boulders, evidence of past human occupation comes to light in rudimentary stone huts, standing stones and the occasional small hill-fort. What was acceptable to prehistoric man, who perhaps found safety in the secluded hollows of the hills, did not appeal in later centuries when the area was abandoned in favour of the richer coastal lowlands. Tracks through this mountain fastness still remained in use, especially those which made use of the low cols breaking the continuity of the Rhinog range. One favoured route lay along the valley of the Afon Artro, passing the placid waters of Llyn Cwm Bychan, before having to negotiate the more difficult climb to skirt the northern slopes of Rhinog Fawr. It is still possible to follow this route today even to the extent of reaching Cwm Bychan lake by car.

From Cwm Bychan a pleasant walk through the woods leads to the paved causeway, long known as the Roman Steps. Great slabs of flagstones which litter the surrounding hillsides have been placed to form a dry and well-marked route to the summit col. But were the Romans responsible for laying the 2,000 or more great slabs? Recent opinion takes the view that the Roman Steps is a misnomer, and the paved way dates only from the medieval period, possibly as part of an essential supply route to the castle town of Harlech. In later centuries, possibly after the importance of Harlech had diminished, the route continued to be used by teams of packhorses making their way across country to Bala and beyond.

But even if we dismiss the idea that the Romans were the original builders of the paved way this does not necessarily mean that they did not use the line of the track through the Rhinogs. Only a few miles away to the east lay one of their main north-south lines of communications in this part of Wales with the fortress of Tomen-y-Mur as a principal defensive strongpoint. It is likely that in maintaining this route the Roman legions did make the occasional sally down to the coast using this track through the Rhinogs. So although the 'steps' may not be Roman, the route which they later marked might well have felt the tramp of Roman soldiers or their paid mercenaries.

The ascent from Cwm Bychan (easily reached by car) first leads through a deciduous wood and then reaches open country with scrubby thorns and poor pasture

(below left) The Roman Steps crossing the Harlech Dome

The slabs used in the building of the track were taken from the many flat boulders which litter the adjacent slopes of the Rhinogs. They represent the product of ice erosion which prised them from the bare rock outcrops and then rafted them to lower levels

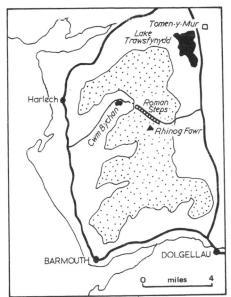

Further reading: Condry, W. *Snowdonia National Park* (Collins, 1966)

Medieval planned town: Winchelsea, Sussex

Winchelsea is a pleasant quiet place today. Attractive, unspectacular Georgian and Victorian houses occupy the medieval burgage plots, sheep crop the grass closely across the lines of vanished medieval streets and the huge unfinished church of St Thomas, a chancel without a nave, stands as a memorial to the years in the 1330s when New Winchelsea's prosperity began to trickle away.

The original Winchelsea

Winchelsea or New Winchelsea bears one of the oldest names among English towns. There was a town and a port, on

The incomplete church at Winchelsea represents the high ambitions of the planners of Edward I's new town that failed to come to fruition. The church occupies one of the thirty-nine *insulae* that composed the original grid-iron plan

The design of the new town of Winchelsea

Iham, the site above the levels of the Brede valley that Edward I purchased for the laying out of New Winchelsea in the 1280s

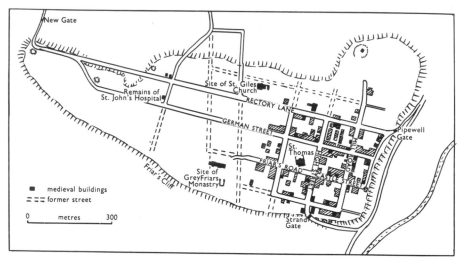

a site now lost to the seaward of Rye, before the Norman Conquest. It was collecting tolls from the traffic of its port in the reign of Canute and a silver coin of Edgar's time, with the inscription *Wencles* or Winchelsea, suggests that a mint was already established there in the tenth century. The foundation of New Winchelsea by Edward I in 1280 was prompted by a succession of storms in the middle decades of the thirteenth century that ultimately led to the abandonment and destruction of the more ancient town. Severe storms in the Channel in the 1250s and again in the 1280s drastically changed the coastline of Romney Marsh. Shingle ridges to the eastward of Rye

76

were broken through and the diversion of the Rother into a new channel to the south of Dungeness made the site of Old Winchelsea untenable. Today its location, somewhere under the sea off Camber, is not known with any certainty.

New Winchelsea

In the closing years of the thirteenth century, Winchelsea was built afresh on the low summit of a cliff-edged hill above the river Brede. Edward I purchased the manor of Iham and the score or so of houses that made up its village for the laying out of a new town, in 1280. The planning of New Winchelsea was placed in the hands of three men, the Warden of the Cinque Ports, a rich merchant, Henry le Waleys, and Itier Bochard, a native of south-west France, who had worked on the building of new towns in that region. Under the guidance of the latter the new town of Winchelsea was shaped. Its main streets, laid out to a width of 50ft (15m), and the lanes that crossed at right angles made a formal chess-board pattern, a grid-iron plan. Thirty-nine rectangular plots between the regular network of roads were sketched out for development. The town was never finished. Only twelve quarters out of the thirty-nine were built over. A busy period of growing commerce in the decades about 1300 was followed by a sharp decline by the middle of the fourteenth century. The Bailiff's Accounts of 1342 list ninety-four houses in New Winchelsea as uninhabited Edward I's new town that had been reluctantly occupied by the merchant burgesses of Old Winchelsea after a severe winter storm of 1288 was eclipsed by its better placed rival, the port and borough of Rye.

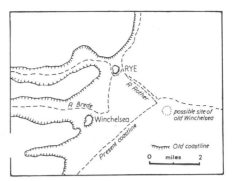

Coastal changes associated with the founding of New Winchelsea in the late thirteenth century

Winchelsea from the air shows the formal grid-iron plan of a medieval new town

Further reading: Millward, R. and Robinson, A. H. W. *South-East England: The Channel Coastlands* (Macmillan, 1973)

Norman castle town: Ludlow, Shropshire

One of the most remarkable features of the high Middle Ages in Europe is the foundation of hundreds of new towns. Ludlow, dating from the closing years of the eleventh century, is about the most perfect example of this theme in landscape history. The castle, built over several generations by the de Lacys and the Mortimers, crowns the bluff above the river Teme that served as a quarry. St Lawrence's church lies beyond the market place

The century that followed the Norman Conquest of England in 1066 saw the founding of many castles. We have it on the authority of the Domesday Book, compiled in 1086, that in existing towns houses were destroyed and buildings demolished to make way for the castle. This happened, for example, at Lincoln and Norwich. At many other places the building of a castle in the years about 1100 heralded the birth of a new town. Ludlow was one of the most successful of the castle-towns of the Welsh border country. It is still a busy regional centre with a population of almost 7,000. Some of its neighbours among the scarped and wooded hills of south Shropshire and Herefordshire — Richard's Castle, Wigmore, Clun and Bishop's Castle — had similar origins as strategic boroughs, but over the centuries they have failed to retain their urban functions.

Castle and town at Ludlow seem to have come into being at the same time in the closing years of the eleventh century. Roger de Lacy began the construction of the castle's great keep on a limestone bluff above the bend of the river Teme in 1085. In the following decade, while masons quarried the cliff face for limestone to build the encircling wall of the inner bailey, the nameless planners and Norman architects were employed in laying out the streets of a Norman town across the gentle slopes of the ground at the castle gate.

Architectural development

Ludlow has the typical rectangular street-plan of so many of the towns that came into existence in western Europe between 1100 and 1300. The key to the town plan is the wide, rectangular High Street that stretched along the ridge-top, above the Teme, between the castle and the parish church of St Lawrence. Three wide parallel streets, Old Street, Broad Street and Mill Street, run at right angles to the main axis down the gentle slopes to the river. The rectangular grid-iron plan was completed by a pattern of parallel connecting lanes. Castle and town evolved through the Middle Ages. The Lacy family ruled at Ludlow until 1306 when their territorial possessions passed to that most powerful family of marcher lords, the Mortimers. During the middle years of the twelfth century Gilbert de Lacy built the little chapel of St Mary Magdalene in the castle's inner bailey. It has a circular nave after the shape of the church of the Holy Sepulchre at Jerusalem. Fifty years later, Hugh de Lacy built the huge curtain wall that encloses the outer bailey of the castle and in extending its area by four times was forced to encroach on the western flank of the town. Early in the fourteenth century Roger de Mortimer completed the main building of the castle with a range along the north wall that contained the Great Hall. The main achievement of the citizens of Ludlow was the rebuilding of the church of St Lawrence in the fifteenth century, a time of high prosperity in the cloth trade.

Further reading: Millward, R. and Robinson, A. H. W. *The Welsh Marches* (Macmillan, 1971)

Symmetry in the town plan of Ludlow

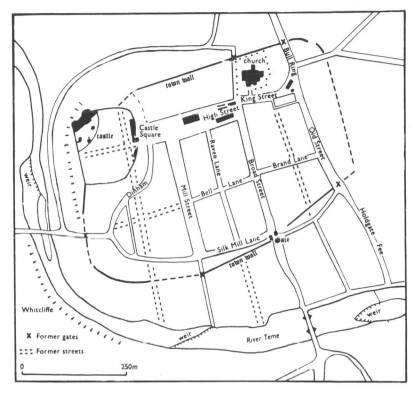

Ludlow Castle seen above the medieval quarry from the Teme

79

Silted sea strait: the Wantsum Channel, Kent

The eastern end of the sea strait which existed in Roman times was guarded by the fortress of Richborough. In the defensive enclosure formed of massive flint walls there is a concrete cross, variously described as the base for a monument or a lighthouse

Flemish weavers brought considerable prosperity to the town of Sandwich, a leading member of the Cinque Port confederation. New styles of architecture were also introduced and existed side-by-side with the more traditional Wealden buildings. Many survive in Sandwich especially in the street known as The Strand

The original sea strait

When the Romans under Julius Caesar landed on the Kent shores during their reconnaissance expeditions of 55 and 54BC, they must have found a coastline very different from that of today. There was no great shingle foreland like Dungeness thrusting out into the deep waters of the English Channel and no Romney Marsh behind, while farther north the Isle of Thanet was a true island. Following the successful campaigns of Claudius from AD43 onwards, Roman galleys used the quiet waters of this sea strait of the Wantsum Channel as they made their way towards London. Some measure of the importance which the Romans attached to the route can be seen from the fact that substantial fortresses were built at each end: Richborough in the east and Reculver to control the northern approach. Both survive today in a ruinous state although it is still possible to appreciate their strategic position even in terms of a much changed landscape.

Development in medieval times

The Wantsum Channel, formed out of a natural hollow in the chalk, was gradually silting up even in Roman times. At its eastern end, close to the present town of Sandwich, a great barrier of shingle known as the Stonar Bank (now used by the main Sandwich to Ramsgate road) had already been thrown up and this undoubtedly encouraged the development of mud-flats and banks of sand behind it. Even so the strait continued to be used right up to the tenth century. As time went on the mud-flats gradually became covered with salt-loving vegetation similar to that occurring on the shores of Pegwell Bay today.

By early medieval times, there was salt-marsh ripe for reclamation. Much of the marsh belonged to St Augustine's Priory at Canterbury and it was under the control of this religious house that considerable areas of land were reclaimed from the twelfth century onwards.

Walls, often of stones and sand, were built to keep out any exceptionally high tides and they still survive around Minster and Stonar where they retain their names of Sea Wall and Monk's Wall. At the northern end of the former sea strait one wall, named after Cardinal Morton, must date from about 1486 and this took in a large parcel of land around St Nicholas. The final closure of the northern entrance did not take place until the end of the eighteenth century and with it the last remnant of the Wantsum Channel disappeared.

Further reading: Millward, R. and Robinson, A. H. W. *South East England: The Channel Coastlands* (Macmillan, 1973)

The quay at Sandwich, once the thriving commercial core of the medieval port but now only serving the occasional fishing vessel and the more common pleasure craft

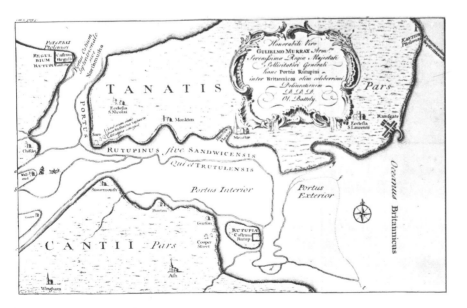

The Wantsum Channel in medieval times

Failed medieval town: Stogursey, Somerset

Some medieval new towns succeeded, many failed. In the foreground is Priory Farm and the dovecote, all that remains apart from the twelfth-century church, of the priory. The middle distance shows the market place, the chief clue in the present landscape to the attempt to make a new town in the twelfth century

The core of the priory that was dissolved in 1414. The church, its style most eccentric among Somerset's parish churches, was probably raised by nameless masons brought from Normandy

The English landscape contains scores of towns in embryo, places that were founded as markets and boroughs between the Norman Conquest and the closing years of the thirteenth century that have never grown through the first-stage of their urban development. Today they are no more than villages, but in their layouts and buildings they often betray the high ambitions that attended their beginnings some eight centuries ago.

Stogursey lies in west Somerset in a quiet, little-disturbed countryside to the north of the long, gentle crest of the Quantock Hills. The second element of the placename perpetuates the memory of the Norman family of de Courcy who acquired this Somerset manor of Stoke after the Conquest. They have long since vanished from the scene but there is little doubt that the de Courcy family tried to raise their newly acquired Somerset property to the status of a

borough. No document survives to prove that Stogursey ever received a borough charter, but the fact that in the Middle Ages a weekly market and two annual fairs were held here suggests that it had acquired some of the necessary economic functions of a town. Even more convincing is the evidence that the place once sent two members to a medieval parliament, a privilege commonly associated with boroughs. Late in the eleventh century the de Courcys built a castle at Stogursey; perhaps this was the first act in the transformation of the village of Stoke into a market town. Today its most impressive feature is the circular moat that was made by an artificial diversion of the brook. Of the little medieval town itself only the quiet market square and the long narrow garden plots of its former burgess houses betray a former pretension to borough status.

The de Courcys introduced another alien element into the history of Stogursey when, about the year 1107, they granted the church of St Andrew and its tithes to the Benedictine abbey of Lonlay in Normandy. Early in the twelfth century the monks built a priory at Stogursey and rebuilt the parish church to serve the inhabitants of the nascent borough and their own small community that was established on the outskirts of the town on rising land

across the Stogursey Brook. In 1414, at the time of long and bitter wars with France, the priory was closed with many other daughter cells of the great Norman abbeys. But 300 years of monasticism are not totally obliterated from Stogursey's landscape. Priory Farm occupies the site of the former monastic buildings, and is built largely from its stones. A thatched circular dovecote remains and the twelfth-century church with its central tower probably was the work of some unknown architect from Normandy.

The site of Stogursey mill that stood beside the castle of the de Courcys

Further reading: Millward, R. and Robinson, A. H. W. *The South West Peninsula* (Macmillan, 1971)

Medieval cloth town: Lavenham, Suffolk

Lavenham's great medieval wool-church was raised in the fifteenth century amid the peaceful Suffolk countryside

Lavenham is without compare among England's medieval towns that have survived into the present day. Accounts written about the turn of the twentieth century tell of the shabby state of its timbered medieval houses and of the richly carved Guildhall on the Market Square with its smashed and broken windows, forgotten and neglected. All that is changed now. Lavenham's chief occupation is tourism, although a threat of settling a few hundred of London's overspill population as well as the establishment of new industries has been held out in one regional planning scheme for Suffolk.

The peak of Lavenham's medieval prosperity was reached in the fifteenth

century. From the closing years of the fourteenth until the middle of the sixteenth century it was a busy centre of cloth-making, producing the coarse-textured kerseys that took their name from a neighbouring village. The visual perfection of Lavenham, a museum specimen of a late medieval industrial settlement, rests on the fact that after the extinction of the cloth trades nothing of commercial importance came to take its place. Lost among the byways of West Suffolk's rich countryside, Lavenham survived as an agricultural settlement with a lingering industrial occupation of spinning yarn for the weavers of Norwich, an activity that was extinct by the early years of the nineteenth century.

The little town that sprawls across a shallow valley separating the hill-top sites of the Market Place and the parish church bears all the marks of its brief decades of high prosperity. Each street contains timber-framed houses from these times. Some have the characteristic projection 'oversailing' of the first floors. Others, particularly in the late sixteenth and early seventeenth centuries had their structures hidden behind smooth, palely coloured plaster finishes; rarely these have been elaborately decorated with patterns in relief — a technique peculiar to East Anglia known as pargetting.

The focal points in an architectural exploration of Lavenham are the Market Place with its highly ornate Guildhall of the Guild of Corpus Christi that was built in 1529, and the parish church. The latter, among England's finest village churches, stands as a memorial to Lavenham's age of prosperity. Its unity of style, wholly a Late Perpendicular church, tells of an intensive half century of building between 1480 and 1530. The patrons of this splendid church, built in the local flint and limestone imported from Northamptonshire, were John de Vere, 13th Earl of Oxford, lord of the manor of Lavenham,

and the rich clothiers of the town. Outstanding among them was the Spring family who contributed the building of the 140ft (45m) tower, a landmark from miles around. The Spring Chapel, memorial brasses and the coat of arms of Thomas Spring as well as numerous shields of the de Vere family enliven the detail of Lavenham parish church and remind one of its merchant origins at the end of the fifteenth century.

Further reading: Scarfe, N. *Suffolk — The Making of the English Landscape* (Hodder, 1973)

The rich clothiers of Lavenham in the closing decades of the fifteenth century built one of the finest of late Perpendicular churches in England, a permanent symbol of the most prosperous age in the history of this Suffolk wool town. It is built of local flint and Northamptonshire limestone

Lavenham is rich in timber-framed houses, the homes of late medieval clothier families

Fourteenth-century peat diggings: the Broads, Norfolk

Barton Broad with its strings of islets which represent the former causeways to the peat-diggings prior to flooding

The wide expanses of open water linked by sluggish rivers like the Bure and Ant lying to the north-east of Norwich represent man's greatest modifications to the natural landscape ever accomplished in this country. Such is the scale of the whole undertaking that even twenty years ago it was looked upon as impossible and the origin of the Broads was sought in terms of natural processes. Research by a team of experts including an historical geographer, a botanist and geomorphologist has shown that the Broads are no less than flooded medieval peat-workings dug out by man.

Much of the evidence has come from the records of St Benet's Abbey, set in a lonely spot beside the river Bure. The earliest reference dates from the twelfth century when certain areas in Hoveton

Peat-digging as well as sedge-cutting for thatching is still carried out though not on the scale of the past

parish were set aside for peat-digging. In one year these diggings yielded no fewer than a million turves. As activity on this scale went on over a wide area for more than 200 years, it is perhaps not surprising that huge basins were excavated covering about 2,600 acres in all. Demand was especially heavy in the nearby city of Norwich, a very important centre in the Middle Ages. The priory kitchens alone used nearly 400,000 turves in a single year. Most were carried by cart along a maze of minor roads, though some went by water.

The conversion of a peat-cutting into a broad resulted from a gradual flooding over a long period of time. There are records of a lake existing at South Walsham in 1315, and by the end of the century peat-cutting had virtually stopped in this area. Elsewhere it went on longer and even when the peat was under water a special rake, with a bag net called a dydle, was used to dredge the peat from the floor of the man-made lake. The main reason for the flooding was that from about the thirteenth century onwards there was a change in the relative levels of land and sea. Coastal areas and low-lying river valleys were now increasingly at risk. By the

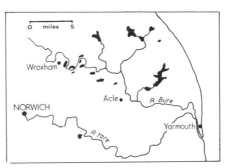

The principal areas of broads in the Norfolk landscape

A Broadland farm cottage with thatched roof from local sedge though the outbuildings use pantiles, another common roofing material in East Anglia

fifteenth century working had become so difficult that the flooded peat-cuttings were no longer profitable and had to be abandoned. What was the medieval peat-diggers' loss has been the tourists' gain for in the past thirty years the Broads have become increasingly popular for boating and sailing.

Further reading: Ellis, E. A. *The Broads* (Collins, 1965)

87

Pennine field patterns: Chelmorton, Derbyshire

Chelmorton is the highest parish in England. Its simple plan, a street of farmhouses, is hemmed in by the network of white, limestone walls that marks out the site of former open fields. At the top of the picture where slopes climb steeply to the plateau above the church, one can see the large formal rectangles of the fields that were enclosed from the common in 1809

At more than 1,000ft (300m) above sea-level Chelmorton has long claimed to be the highest parish in England. It occupies a wide shallow basin in the Carboniferous Limestone plateau of central Derbyshire. The village, a collection of thirteen farms and a number of cottages, is gathered along a lane that leads gently down from the parish church. Around this 'street' settlement a web of limestone walls makes a patchwork of squares and rectangles across the fresh green countryside marking out the fields of Chelmorton's farmers. Two field patterns are immediately evident as we survey the lands of the parish from the steep slopes of Chelmorton Low. In the immediate foreground and middle distance the long straight walls, placed close together and in parallel, form a pattern of narrow rectangular fields.

A seventeenth-century map, drawn in 1638 as a preparation for the enclosure of the Royal Forest of the Peak, shows the acres to the north and west of the village as Chelmorton Field. It is believed that this was once an open field whose strips were shared and farmed in common by the inhabitants of Chelmorton.

The time when open-field farming began at Chelmorton is a total mystery.

Chelmorton's great field that was enclosed at some unknown date. Access lanes lead between the high, limestone walls that hedge the narrow rectangular-shaped fields. In the distance the limestone plateau shows patchy blocks of woodland, plantations made by the Dukes of Devonshire in an attempt to tame the bleak landscape on the outskirts of Buxton

open acres would form the 'infield' — land that was almost continuously cultivated with arable crops, largely oats and rye, and kept in heart with the dung of livestock.

Beyond the limits of the open field encircling limestone hills provided acres of common grazing for sheep and cattle, a place too where the parishioners of Chelmorton tried their luck in the search for lead ore. The commons of Chelmorton were enclosed by Act of Parliament in 1805 and 1809. The field patterns determined by the surveyors under the terms of the enclosure award are completely different from those that resulted from the earlier enclosure of the open field. Large square-shaped fields with scattered planted spinneys now mark out the site of the former common grazings.

Further reading: Millward, R. and Robinson, A. H. W. *The Peak District* (Eyre Methuen, 1975)

There are no clues to the date of its enclosure and the method of farming its communally held acres is far from certain. Traditionally, open-field farming systems have been associated with the settlement of the English lowlands by the Anglo-Saxons after the beginning of the fifth century. The Anglian colonisation of the Peak District came late in time; Chelmorton's field may have been sketched out between AD600 and 800. But it is also possible that open-field farming in the Peak District may be associated with the pre-Saxon occupants of the southern Pennines, the British. It has been argued that medieval Chelmorton practised an 'infield-outfield' system of farming. The

Five Wells, Taddington. The next parish to Chelmorton contains the relics of a late Neolithic chambered tomb — a burial place some 4,000 years old. It provides striking evidence that the limestone plateau of north Derbyshire provided one of the rare attractive environments for the settlement of early man in highland Britain

Deserted village: Great Stretton, Leicestershire

England's 'lost' villages

Local history research since the 1940s has shown that the English countryside contains the sites of hundreds of deserted villages. Grassy platforms, the faint hollows of former fishponds and shallow green tracks that trace out the lines of long-abandoned streets and lanes are all that we see today. At some places the record on the ground has become so faint that the presence of a medieval village community can be found only in documents from the fourteenth century and earlier. By 1968, careful research exploring the field evidence and combing the documentary record had counted 2,263 lost villages in England alone. In some counties the figure runs into hundreds. Lincolnshire has 220 deserted sites and there are known to be 148 in Norfolk and 128 in Warwickshire.

Leicestershire contains 67 deserted villages. One, Ingarsby, probably had a population of about 150 when the manor was granted to Leicester Abbey in 1352. A little more than a century later Ingarsby was totally deserted and its population driven from the land. The whole manor was turned into a pasture for sheep.

One of Leicestershire's three score of deserted villages. We can see the sunken lanes and the raised, grassy platforms that mark the foundations of buildings. Beyond the bounds of the village the character-istic pattern of ridge-and-furrow marks the site of Ingarsby's former open fields

Great Stretton

Great Stretton, a romantic site lying beside the Roman road, the Gartree Lane, leading southward from the city of Leicester, presents a complex story of desertion. Today Great Stretton is represented by a lonely church with a low squat tower and the familiar grassy platforms and hollow-ways of a deserted village. At the southern edge a big rectangular mound surrounded by a deep grass-grown moat marks the site of the medieval manor house. The earliest clue to Great Stretton's desertion is con-tained in a will of 1500. It mentions the 'inclosures and approvements' that Thomas Kebell made on his property at Great Stretton — part of the manor, most likely some 200 acres (80ha), that have since formed the Stretton Hall

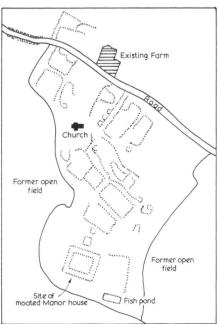

Relict features of the former village of Great Stretton

estate, had been enclosed from the open fields in the last quarter of the fifteenth century. Most of the settlement survived through the Tudor decades practising a traditional system of farming in the intermixed strips of open fields. By the mid-seventeenth century much enclosure had taken place at Great Stretton and pasture farming had extended. The parish registers of the 1660s show a greatly diminished population — a village community set on a course for extinction. A century later only two farms were left and the church had fallen into ruins, to be re-roofed and made good again in 1838.

The main causes of desertion in the Middle Ages

When the growing cloth industry gave rise to a great demand for wool, manorial lords discovered the profits to be made from enclosing their land on a large scale for sheep farming. Whole villages were left to ruin, for the peasants were evicted from their homes to facilitate the exclusive use of the land for sheep-grazing. Many of Leicestershire's villages had vanished by the end of the fifteenth century largely under this pressure. The Black Death was also a contributing factor to the sudden depopulation in the fourteenth century, for this vast epidemic wiped out whole settlements at a time, and perhaps aided the depopulation of around 1,000 villages in England. The main epidemic occurred 1348-9 with recurrences until 1400, by which time the country's population was half of that a hundred years earlier.

Further reading: Hoskins, W. G. *Leicestershire — The Making of the English Landscape* (Hodder & Stoughton, 1957)
Beresford, M. and Hurst, J. G. *Deserted Medieval Villages* (Lutterworth Press, 1971)

The desertion of Great Stretton was a piecemeal process over three centuries. The church survived as a building to be restored in 1838

Sheep graze the pastures beside the lane, now a green hollow-way, that once led past the church to the village at Great Stretton

Planned industrial village: Gatehouse-of-Fleet, Kircudbright

(right) Gatehouse-of-Fleet set amid the pleasant countryside of the north shore of the Solway Firth, a countryside enriched by the improving landlords, James Murray of Cally and his son, Alexander, who founded and developed the industrial settlement

(below) From the middle of the eighteenth century the Industrial Revolution was to generate hundreds of new settlements. Gatehouse-of-Fleet, an industrial village with its simple grid-iron plan of streets based on the Military Road through south-west Scotland, depended upon water power. After 1850 its textile industries had become extinct

South-west Scotland with its wild granite uplands and deeply penetrating bays of the Solway Firth was one of the remotest regions of Britain until it was opened up by road building towards the end of the eighteenth century. One incentive to the development of the area was its position in communications between Carlisle and northern Ireland. In 1642, a time of rebellion in Ireland, the inn at Gatehouse, close by the crossing of the river Fleet, was established as a posting station on the route between Carlisle and Portpatrick. By 1765 the Military Road had been constructed through Galloway to Portpatrick and it crossed the head of the Fleet estuary at Gatehouse.

At the time of the completion of the Military Road, James Murray, owner of Cally Park and one of the foremost among the landed gentry of Galloway, began the development of an industrial village on his estate at Gatehouse. The

first stage of industrial growth, up to 1785, arose out of the resources and needs of the local countryside around the Fleet and saw the opening of a brewery, a tannery and a soapworks. In 1785 an important step forward was taken at Gatehouse when James Murray leased land beside the river, above the bridge of Fleet, to Birtwhistle & Sons, a firm of Yorkshire cattle dealers, for the building of a cotton-spinning mill. Before the end of the century a complex of mills, all busy with cotton spinning or weaving, had gathered by the river. Another factory, owned by Scott & Son, an Ulster firm, had been established at the eastern end of the village, close to the entrance to Cally Park. By 1794 Gatehouse-of-Fleet was employing an industrial population of more than 500. Half a century later, in the 1850s, textile manufacturing died here. The mills fell into ruins; one of them, converted to a bobbin factory, continued working until the 1930s.

Gatehouse, with its rigid grid-iron plan of streets aligned on the Military

Road is a marvellously preserved example of an industrial settlement from the first decades of the Industrial Revolution when water was the chief source of power — the direction of its growth lay in the hands of rich improving landlords, James Murray of Cally and his son, Alexander. Alexander Murray left his mark on the pleasant landscape of the Fleet estuary when he planned the straightening of the winding channel of the Fleet for almost a mile below the settlement. The new cut was made in 1824 with the help of 200 Irish peasants from Murray's estates in Donegal. It is said that most of them were in arrears of rent. Vessels of 150 tons (151 tonnes) could then reach the Old Harbour below Fleet Bridge and ten years later a local shipowner, David McAdam, had Port Macadam built at the head of the canal.

Further reading: Donnachie, I. and Macleod, I. *Old Galloway* (David & Charles, 1974)

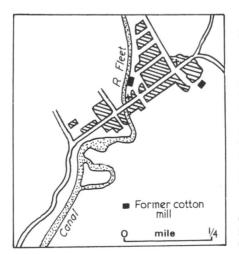

(top) A former water-powered textile mill

A contemporary sketch shows two mills side-by-side with their huge waterwheels using the same source of power. Today, scarcely anything remains in the landscape of the mills that gave life to Gatehouse-of-Fleet in the first half of the nineteenth century

Gatehouse-of-Fleet, a planned industrial village based on cotton factories

Nineteenth-century reclamation: Exmoor, Somerset

of moorland in this ancient royal forest. Three years later the Crown had found a purchaser for the greater part of its Exmoor lands in John Knight, a Midland ironmaster, who acquired an estate of 15,000 acres (6,070ha). John Knight and his son Frederic, who took over the management of the Exmoor lands in 1841, founded fifteen different farms within the 29 mile-long (46km) perimeter wall that fenced in their moorland property. Warren Farm was carved out of the rough moorland on a southward-facing bench above the Exe in 1848. It is one of half a dozen holdings that were brought into being between 1840 and 1850. Frederic Knight was his own architect for these drab courtyard farms built of the dark-grey local rock. High earth banks enclose the rectangular-shaped fields. Along with the shelter belts of conifers and other features of the modern landscape they commemorate the enterprise of the Knight family in taming this upland wilderness.

Simonsbath in the heart of Exmoor was the only settlement in this ancient royal forest when it was purchased by the Midland ironmaster, John Knight, in 1818. The plantations and the regular pattern of field boundaries were part of the reclamation of Exmoor that occupied the Knight family for most of the nineteenth century

Exmoor is one of the chief uplands of south-west England. The greater part of its rolling plateau surface lies at more than 1,000ft (300m) above sea level while some of the highest tracts, as at the source of the River Exe, reach almost 1,600ft (486m). Exmoor's rivers flow in valleys deeply sunk in the sandstone plateau. The Exe, here an infant stream, lies almost 300ft (100m) below the rounded upper edge of its valley slope.

At the beginning of the nineteenth century Exmoor was an unreclaimed wilderness that grazed thousands of sheep through the summer months. In 1816, it is recorded that 25,000 sheep were pastured there from fifty parishes in the surrounding lowlands of Devon and Somerset. But already events had been set in train that were to change the face of this uninhabited upland by the middle of the century. In 1815 an Act of Parliament had been secured to enclose some 25,000 acres (10,117ha)

In the course of the first half of the nineteenth century fifteen new farms were carved out of the wilderness of Exmoor by the Knight family in the development of their **15,000 acre (6,070ha) estate. High earth banks planted with beeches enclosed the rectangular-shaped fields**

Nature too has left a dramatic imprint on the scenery of Exmoor. In August 1952 a prolonged rainstorm of tropical severity caused disastrous floods in the valleys draining from Exmoor. On one of the highest parts of the upland, the Chains at the source of the Exe, 9in (23cm) of rain fell in the space of 5 hours. The scars of this natural disaster that swept away roads and bridges in the region may still be seen in the bared gashes and rumpled ground of landslips on the slopes of the upper Exe around Warren Farm.

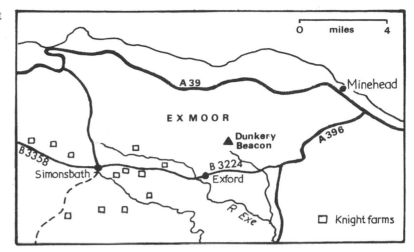

Further reading: Orwin, C. S. *The Reclamation of Exmoor Forest* (David & Charles, 1970)

The farms founded by the Knight family on the wastes of Exmoor

The upper Exe valley, looking towards the Chains where 9in (23cm) of rain fell on an August day of 1952 to set off the disastrous Exmoor flood

Canal landscape: Braunston, Northamptonshire

The former canal warehouse at Braunston now used for boat building. Few working barges are now operating on the canal which is largely given over to pleasure craft

The canal age in Britain lasted a mere eighty years, from about 1760 until 1840, yet in that short space of time it has left an indelible imprint on many parts of the country. The Midlands in particular were to feel the full impact of the new age. The hostile topography of the Midlands created problems and great flights of locks were sometimes needed to surmount obstacles. Today they survive, along with the canals them- selves, as living memorials to the skill of the canal engineers and the labours of the navvies who virtually created the whole system by hand.

The birth of the canal system

The era of canal building began with a tremendous flourish when the Duke of Bridgewater commissioned an untutored millwright, James Brindley, to build an artificial waterway from his coal mines at Worsley to the outskirts of Manchester.

Lock and keeper's cottage at the eastern end of Braunston village

Apart from its usefulness as a means of transport, the canal became an object of curiosity and travellers seeking the wonders of the Peak and Lake District were advised to break their journey at Worsley. As one visitor put it: 'The ingenious Mr Brindley has indeed made such improvements in this way as are truly astonishing. At Barton Bridge he has erected a navigable canal in the air; for it is as high as the tops of trees.' This was only a beginning and during the next fifty years the whole transport system was revolutionised, the way of life for thousands altered, new townships created and an entirely different pattern of architectural and engineering achievement set in motion.

Set astride the watershed of England the Midlands had not been able to take advantage of rivers to carry bulk commodities. Yet with the Industrial Revolution beginning to make itself felt the Birmingham region needed water links with the Mersey, Severn and Thames. It was not until the 1790s that the final network was forged with the creation of a short through-route to London. Various stretches of canal,

owned by different companies, were used and junctions became especially important. At Braunston, where the Grand Junction Canal met the older Oxford Canal, new wharves and basins were built. What was once a sleepy village set in the quiet Northamptonshire countryside suddenly acquired a new lease of life. Warehouses and cottages, plain and utilitarian, sprang up overnight along the canal bank.

Further reading: Hadfield, C. *The Canals of the West Midlands* (David & Charles, 1969)

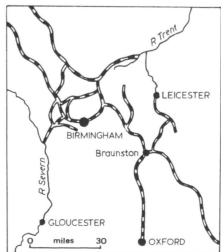

Braunston was formerly an important point of transshipment of cargoes but its canal basins are now taken over entirely by moorings for pleasure boats

The canal system of the Midlands

Copper mountain: Parys, Anglesey

Anglesey is an island of contrasts. Much of it is low-lying with rich pastures carrying large herds of dairy cattle. At intervals the even skyline is abruptly broken by bare hills which rise, often quite precipitously, out of the plain. Parys Mountain, in the north of the island, is typical of these rocky eminences with its long outline seen to be a mass of old mine workings and spoil heaps. Nature endowed Parys with rich deposits of copper, making it unique amongst the Anglesey hills.

Parys was the most famous and productive centre of copper working in the world, in the eighteenth century. Although the Romans scratched the surface mineral deposits it was not until the 1700s that it was realised that in Parys there was a virtual mountain of copper. Working began in earnest in 1768 and for the next hundred years the hill was the scene of intense activity, becoming riddled with mine shafts and levels seeking out the profitable veins. At the south-west end a great opencast pit was engineered which effectively hollowed out the core of the hill. Much

Open pits and waste tips now cover most of the surface of Parys Mountain with old mine buildings gradually crumbling into complete decay. The ruins of the old engine-house lie on the eastern side of the hill. Formerly it housed a Cornish pumping engine which attempted to keep the deeper workings dry

Remains of the settling pits where copper was extracted by precipitation from the metal-bearing waters draining the workings

of the ore was concentrated on the spot before being taken by teams of pack-horses to the nearby port of Amlwch for export to Swansea. In less than a generation the whole appearance of the hill was changed, for in addition to the mining operations themselves, fumes from the concentration works effectively killed off the vegetation as well as preventing its regeneration.

Present-day Parys

Even today, a century after the main activity ceased, Parys presents a scene of desolation with deep pits, dangerous shafts and the intensely disturbed ground of the old spoil tips. To appreciate Parys it is essential to visit its 'lunar' landscape on a fine day when the orange, brown, pink, green and yellow hues of the copper ores shine brightly in the sun. Even the lake of the flooded opencast pit becomes a deep ultra-marine as it reflects the light of the sky. In contrast, on a dull day, this is a landscape of desecration and torment when one is made aware of the destruction wrought by the mine

owners as they greedily devoured the rich copper centre of the hill.

Further reading: Rowlands, J. *Copper Mountain* (Anglesey Antiquarian and Field Club, 1961)

The massive quays and jetties of Amlwch give only a slight hint of the former prosperity of the port in the early nineteenth century when it was crowded with coasters loading copper ore en route for Swansea

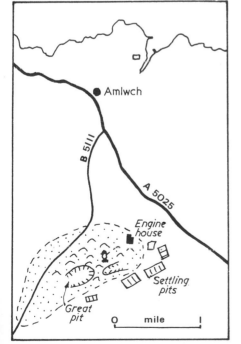

Parys Mountain and its copper-working remains

An artist's impression of the method of working the ore in the early period. Buckets or kibbles were used to haul the ore from the bottom of the great open pit

99

Industrial archeology: Laxey Big Wheel, Isle of Man

Formerly an essential element of the mine activity in the Laxey valley, the great wheel is now probably the greatest single tourist attraction in the Isle of Man

The Laxey Wheel, known as the Lady Isabella from the name of the wife of the governor of the Isle at the time, was brought into use in 1854, and is perhaps the best known industrial monument of a past age in the British Isles. The fame of the Laxey Big Wheel lies in its huge size for it has a diameter of over 70ft (21m).

During the height of the metalliferous mining in the seventeenth and eighteenth centuries great waterwheels like Laxey

were not uncommon in the mining areas of Cornwall, the Lake District and the Pennines. In nearly every case their function was to use running water as a source of power to drain the deep workings of the mines. The Laxey Wheel, working on the overshot principle, generated the equivalent of 200hp.

For all its attraction it must be remembered that the Laxey Wheel came into use at a time when the method was dying out elsewhere.

Competition from the more manageable steam pumps had led to the virtual extinction of huge waterwheels by the latter half of the nineteenth century. In the Isle of Man, dependent on imported coal but with a superfluity of water power from small streams draining the eastern slopes of Snaefell, the situation was slightly different, and this undoubtedly caused the owners of the Laxey mines to persist with an outdated, though still feasible system of power generation. There can be no doubt that the big wheel was a success, and in the latter half of the nineteenth century it made its own distinctive contribution to the considerable output attained by the mines of the Laxey Valley.

Production began in earnest after 1848 although small-scale working had been taking place for up to a century earlier. By 1854 the Laxey mines were producing more zinc blende than the combined output of all the other mines in the British Isles. Production reached its peak in 1875. Zinc blende, lead and silver were obtained to an estimated value of over £90,000 at this time. Output of this order could not be maintained once the richer veins were exhausted and new sources became more difficult to locate. After 1890, the mines gradually became less profitable and were finally closed down in 1919. Miraculously the Big Wheel was not dismantled and has proved capable of restoration to its original working state.

Further reading: Garrad, L. S. *The Industrial Archaeology of the Isle of Man* (David & Charles, 1972)

Little remains in the present landscape to indicate the once bustling activity in the Laxey valley save for the Lady Isabella Wheel with its 70ft (21m) diameter.

China-clay workings: St Austell, Cornwall

The area on the edge of Hensbarrow Down near St Austell presents an unreal appearance with the landscape completely altered with deep pits from which the china clay is won, and the conical heaps of waste sterilising vast areas of ground. Tiny patches of cultivated land still remain in between but most of the countryside has been given over to the profitable clay industry

(right) Old and new workings lie side-by-side. Pumping houses, dating from the time when Cornish engines were used to keep the pits free from water, still hang precariously near the edge of the deep holes.

Even areas far removed from our industrial belts have felt the impact of man as he has exploited the earth's resources. In the South-West Peninsula the most obvious sign of this at the present time is the result of china-clay working. This is centred around the granite upland, for the clay is derived from the decomposition of granite. One of the largest areas of industry is on Hensbarrow Down, close to St Austell. Great holes have been opened up with the huge conical mounds of waste around them. These so dominate the landscape that they have become known as 'The Cornish Alps'. For over 5,000 years man has been shaping the land so that little now remains that could be termed strictly 'natural'. The clearance of woodland in upland Britain and its

replacement by hill pastures or moorland is but one example. Perhaps more obvious is the effect of the search for minerals and other deposits of economic value.

The industry can trace its beginning to 1750 when a Quaker, William Cookworthy, found deposits of clay near Helston which he thought might be suitable for making pottery. Similar clays were later found near St Austell and it was here that the industry became firmly established. Local families like the Rashleighs were prominent in the early years of development. Not only did they control the workings but they also built roads to transport the clay to the coast where it could be shipped to other parts of Britain. Sir Charles Rashleigh also built the port of Charlestown and, although it was used for exporting the local copper and tin deposits, it quickly became the main outlet for the china clay. An inn and rows of cottages around the solid harbour basin were built from 1791 onwards when the harbour was opened.

The cottages that still survive in their various pastel colours add to the adornment of what is naturally an impressive coastline. Although Charlestown still exports the odd cargo of clay, the main centre is now at Par, 2 miles (3km) away to the east. Unlike the copper and tin industries which have long ceased to be important china clay is still very much in demand, and with plentiful deposits available on the granite moors of Hensbarrow the future of the industry looks assured and the Cornish Alps seem likely to grow even larger.

Further reading: Millward, R. and Robinson, A. H. W. *The South West Peninsula* (Macmillan, 1971)

(top) The china-clay working areas of the South-West Peninsula

(bottom) Charlestown, a small artificial port built at a point on the coast nearest the early workings, still retains its early nineteenth-century character with a row of multi-coloured cottages overlooking the loading chutes. Outside the harbour the sea is a milky white from the china-clay sediment in suspension

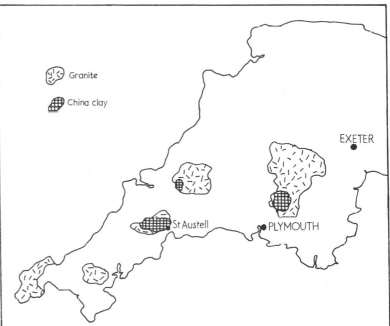

Industrial endowment: the Lower Swansea Valley

Mond Nickel Works at Clydach, established by Ludwig Mond in 1902

Before industry came to this area in the early part of the eighteenth century, the Tawe valley, with Swansea at its mouth, must have presented a pleasant scene. A strip of green meadowland along the flat valley-floor stood out in sharp contrast to the browns and darker hues of the flat-topped hills around. Even as late as 1813 a local man, David Jenkins, could find that, 'The eye of taste had perpetual gratification from the great variety of scenery that presents itself . . . here Nature seems unrivalled in her beauties.' But even as Jenkins wrote, industry was beginning to take its toll of the natural landscape. The copper-smelting works, enticed to the valley by cheap coal hewn from the surrounding hills, was already spreading its polluting wastes over a large area.

The scale of the industry can be measured from the fact that in 1845 the Swansea district was producing 55 per cent of the world's copper. Even when this industry declined, zinc smelting came in to take its place and in 1902 Ludwig Mond established his nickel works at Clydach higher up the valley. The effect of such a heavy concentration of metal industries was dramatic and far-reaching. Apart from the ever-growing waste tips covering the valley floor, the fumes from the works killed off the vegetation to such an extent that even weeds would not grow. Not all the industrialists who came to the Swansea valley were without social conscience. John Morris, for example, a local metal master, built his model town of Morriston on the floor of the valley between 1790 and 1796. He adopted a grid plan with the parish church at the intersection of the two axial streets. The area within the street plan was divided into plots with land enough to graze a cow and grow vegetables. Morriston somehow survived the torments of the nineteenth century though today it shares the desire for rehabilitation like so much of the valley.

The situation in the lower Swansea Valley had deteriorated to such an extent by 1960 that it was no longer possible for the local people to turn their backs on the monstrous eyesore the area had become. A project of research, followed by reclamation, was put in hand and though up to the present the effect has not been spectacular, much has been achieved in what was recognised at the outset to be a costly and time-consuming exercise in land reclamation.

Further reading: Balchin, W. G. V. *Swansea and its Region* (University College, Swansea publication, 1968)

The town of Morriston has, like so much of the valley, changed dramatically since it grew up in the late eighteenth century

Man's folly: Hallsands, Devon

(above) The coastline of Start Bay looking northward from Hallsands, a succession of sandy bays and hard rock headlands

(above right) Cottage ruins are all that remain of the former fishing hamlet, with only the slightest indication of the central street which ran between the individual houses

The siting of Hallsands on the open Start Bay

Of the millions who use our beaches for recreation each summer, few give much thought to the way in which they have been formed and maintained by the sea. Where does the sand or shingle come from? How old are the beach deposits and are they ever likely to disappear altogether as the result of continual stirring up and wearing away by the waves? These questions are difficult to answer but at Hallsands man himself, unknowingly, has provided some clues to help solve the problem.

At the turn of the century, when extensions were being made to Devonport Dockyard, a local contractor was given permission to use the sea-bed deposits of Start Bay for making the concrete. The contractor found that the best shingle was on the beach and so at high tide he brought in his dredger and carried away the material. Altogether he removed upwards of half a million tons and lowered the beach by as much as 15ft (5m) in places. Protests from the local fishermen who lived in the hamlet of Hallsands failed to move the Board of Trade who were responsible for

issuing the licence. At the outset the officials were convinced that the sea would replenish the beach shingle, but when this did not happen they withdrew permission in 1903. By this time the damage had been done and the beach remained in its depleted state. The greatest tragedy came in 1917 when severe easterly gales finally destroyed the fishermen's cottages and led to the abandonment of the hamlet. Time has not healed the ravages of the past and today Hallsands still has a forlorn appearance with only one or two of the original cottages remaining. The beach

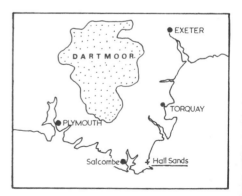

106

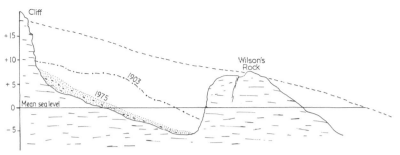

(above) **Changing beach levels at Hallsands due to removal of shingle**

(below) **Hallsands as it appeared in 1897. At that time the fishermen's cottages were safe behind a wide protective beach for even at high water, when this photograph was taken, the sea lay some distance away**

(bottom of page) **The severe storm of January 1917 brought about the final destruction of the village though for some years previously most of the cottages had been damaged each winter**

has not built up since 1903 when operations were finally brought to a halt.

Its most prominent feature is the stack known as Wilson's Rock, formerly completely covered with beach shingle. The fact that the beach has not recovered in the past seventy years is not really surprising in view of the lack of shingle offshore. The question arises as to the source of the shingle in the first place and the assumption must be that when sea level began to rise at the end of the Ice Age, some 12,000 years ago, it swept material before it and then piled it on to the beaches it was in the process of making. Hallsands beach, like so many others around our coasts, is of great antiquity and apparently formed from a once-for-all supply. If this is removed artificially, then, as Hallsands has proved, the consequences can be disastrous and long-lasting.

Further reading: Millward, R. and Robinson, A. H. W. *The South West Peninsula* (Macmillan, 1971)

Derelict land: Bedfordshire claypits

The partly flooded claypit at Stewartby where huge drag-line excavators are removing the material at an alarming rate. A conveyor belt carries the clay directly to the brickworks

The cross-country line from Bedford to Bletchley was of fundamental importance in the original siting of the various brickworks. It served both as a means of importing fuel for the kilns and also transported the finished bricks to various parts of the Home Counties and the Midlands

Extractive industries like open-cast coal mining, stone quarrying and gravel digging have voracious appetites and with modern mechanical equipment they can devour the landscape at an alarming rate. The claypits of the brick companies are one of the worst offenders, in that restoration has proved so costly that only under favourable circumstances is it attempted on a large scale. The brick manufactories themselves represent an intrusion on the landscape with their cluster of tall chimneys dominating the skyline for miles around.

The claypits 'landscape'

The total impact of claypits and works is therefore considerable and nowhere is this better seen than in the broad belt of clay lowland which runs at the foot of the Chilterns through Oxfordshire, Bedfordshire and into Northamptonshire. Fortunately the really large-scale

workings are concentrated so that the disfigurement is confined to certain areas. South of Bedford, near the villages of Stewartby and Marston Mortaine, the brick companies have completely transformed a rural landscape. The attraction of the area lies in the thick beds of grey-green clay which contain up to 10 per cent carbonaceous material so that fuel costs in brickmaking are reduced by almost two-thirds. A considerable thickness of overburden has to be removed and when this is dumped in the pit as the working face recedes it gives rise to rows of conical hillocks which would seem to be more characteristic of the moon's surface than the Bedfordshire countryside. Many of the deeper pits have become flooded so that an additional man-made element is introduced. With the area now supplying almost a fifth of the output of bricks for the whole country, the problem of derelict land increases each year.

The reclamation problem

Very little by way of reclamation has been attempted up to the present time.

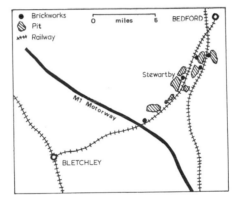

Land restoration has so far proved impossible for pits left in this condition

The brickwork countryside of Bedfordshire straddling the Bedford to Bletchley railway line

The companies argue that the cost of filling in the deep holes would be uneconomic as it would mean bringing material from distant areas. Some of the household rubbish from Bedford is in fact dumped in the old workings but it makes only a small contribution and will never solve the problem. The alternative of bringing waste ash from power stations, such as has been attempted in the Peterborough area, foundered because of the high rail-transport costs involved. The future for the area looks gloomy but the recent use of one of the pits near Stewartby for boating perhaps points the way for the future in this leisure-conscious age.

Further reading: Bugler, J. *Polluting Britain* (Penguin, 1972)

Capital city: Edinburgh

Edinburgh's dramatic site lies amid a group of volcanic hills. In the distance is Arthur's Seat and Salisbury Crags. The foreground is occupied by the formal layout of the New Town while beyond the symmetrical pattern of the roof of Waverley Station is the site of the dark congested medieval town

Among the world's capital cities Edinburgh must possess one of the most dramatic and exciting settings. It occupies the narrow plain of Lothian between the Pentland Hills and the Firth of Forth. A rare feature of Edinburgh's landscape is the little plains, gorges and shapely hills that compose the detailed geography of the city.

Seven volcanic hills rise within the compass of the greater city and at its very heart, determining the growth pattern of the medieval town, lie three closely grouped volcanic crags: Arthur's Seat and Salisbury Crags, Calton Hill, and the Castle Rock. The latter, a plug of volcanic rocks, rises sheer for almost 500ft (150m) at its western end. Its eastern slope, a broad ridge, falls for more than a mile to the site of Holyrood Palace. This ridge, composed of glacial clays, was deposited by eastward moving ice during the Ice Age, in the lee of the sharp volcanic rock that has been a castle-site for almost a thousand years.

It seems likely that settlement on the

Castle Rock goes back into the centuries long before the reign of David I (1124-53) when the medieval town of Edinburgh along the High Street was founded. The name, Edinburgh, most likely descends from a placename, Dun-eideann, in the long extinct Celtic language that was spoken during the Iron Age in Scotland. Dun-eideann, meaning 'the fort of Eidin', appears in a poem of the late sixth century. It suggests that a Dark-Age earthwork, crowning the summit of the Castle Rock, must have been the oldest man-made feature of the city's landscape.

The Old and New Towns

The medieval town took shape in the middle decades of the twelfth century when David established a chartered burgh with its merchants and craftsmen on the long ridge below the castle. At the foot of the ridge, closing the end of Canongate, he founded the Abbey of Holyrood, later to become a royal palace. For almost six centuries Edinburgh remained confined to its hill-top site, hemmed in by a rim of marshes and shallow lakes beneath its volcanic crag. With its steady growth in importance and population, especially in the seventeenth and early eighteenth centuries, the demand for building space was fierce. These centuries shaped the profile of the inner city with its tall buildings, dark stony courtyards and countless narrow alleys or wynds. In the last quarter of the eighteenth century Edinburgh burst its bounds with the founding of the New Town. A spacious Georgian quarter of wide streets, squares and crescents, New Town was designed as a residential district, but soon commerce and business was to drift from the confined quarters of the Old Town on the rock to the surroundings of Princes Street.

Further reading: Youngson, A. J. *The Making of Classical Edinburgh* (Edinburgh University Press, 1966) Keith, D. (ed) *The City of Edinburgh* (Collins, Glasgow, 1966)

The Castle Rock forms the culmination of the High Street, the axis of the medieval town. Although all trace of prehistoric settlement has vanished from the landscape, one interpretation of the name of Edinburgh suggests that the castle was previously occupied by an Iron-Age fort

Princes Street represents the shift of the heart of Edinburgh from the spine of the castle ridge after the development of the New Town

Acknowledgements

For permission to reproduce photographs
we wish to thank the following:
Aerofilms Limited — pages 18 (bottom),
20, 25 (bottom), 26, 38 (top), 41, 46
(top), 60 (top), 60 (bottom), 65, 77, 78,
82, 84, 86, 92, 94, 100, 101, 102, 106,
110, 111 (top).
C. H. Wood (Bradford) Limited — pages
17 (top), 30, 31, 64.
H. Tempest (Cardiff) Limited — pages 16,
24 (top), 72, 73.
Tom Weir, Gartocharn, Dunbartonshire —
pages 18 (top), 40, 54-5, 56, 63.
Lakeland Photographic, Ambleside —
page 21 (bottom).
Peter Baker, Clevedon, Somerset — pages
22 (top), 24 (bottom), 39 (top), 38-9,
62 (top), 62 (bottom), 79, 92-3, 111
(bottom).
Cambridge University Collection — 28,
66, 80 (top), 88-9, 90.
J. Allan Cash Limited — page 58.
Swansea City Council — page 104.
W. Glamorgan Council — page 105.